# THE HISTORICAL ROOTS
## OF THE
# PRESBYTERIAN CHURCH IN AMERICA

A Presbyterian Primer

# THE HISTORICAL ROOTS
# OF THE
# PRESBYTERIAN CHURCH
# IN AMERICA

**Don K. Clements**

Metokos Press
Narrows, VA 24124

Unless otherwise indicated, all Scripture quotations are from
The Holy Bible, English Standard Version, copyright 2001
by Crossway Bibles, a division of Good News Publishers.
Used by permission. All rights reserved.

Published by Metokos Press, Inc., committed to providing materials
easily accessible to the average reader while at the same time
presenting biblical truth from within the framework of biblical and
confessional churches of Reformed and Presbyterian heritage. Visit us
on the web at *www.metokospress.com*.

Cover design by Chip Evans, Walker-Atlanta, Atlanta, GA.

Layout and editing by Diane Hitzfeld, Atlanta, GA.

Printed in the United States by Lightning Source, LaVergne, TN.

ISBN 978-0-9742331-7-8

## Introduction to the Series

Presbyterian Primers is a series of medium-length books, written in a non-academic style that I hope will be accessible to the many people (but especially "guys") in churches who do not regularly read books about "church stuff."

Since my seminary days, I have frequently complained that, in arenas other than Reformed and Presbyterian circles, one could find many books written in such a manner. But the majority of Reformed and Presbyterian related works were either designed as adult Sunday school textbooks (with the expectation of a certain level of understanding that goes with such readers), or were written by academics with the hope that fellow academics and a few academically minded people would buy enough copies to cover the cost of publication. There has seldom been literature designed more specifically to reach new or previously unread church members on topics of importance.

The series will include a growing but not fixed number of titles. Volumes on *Biblical Church Government* and *God the Holy Spirit* are already in print, now joined by *The Historical Roots of the Presbyterian Church in America*. After this volume on church history, others may include titles such as *God the Father, God the Son, Biblical Interpretation, New Geneva Introduction to the Old Testament, New Geneva Introduction to the New Testament,* an introductory (but not systematic) work on the Westminster Confession entitled *Conversations on the Confession,* and perhaps others.

## *Foreword*

The lessons of history are many. On the negative side, those who fail to learn from the mistakes of the past are condemned to repeat them. More positively, the courageous acts of past heroes can inspire us to similar efforts. Most important, indications of the providential purposes of our Lord in the history of the church can encourage us to join our hearts and efforts with those purposes for the good of God's people and the glory of his name.

As Teaching Elder Don Clements indicates in his Preface, he was a student in my course on Reformation and Modern Church History in 1973. It is gratifying to a teacher to find his former student has not only absorbed the content of his teaching profitably, but has gone beyond it in many ways, adding to it and applying it to the on-going life of the church. While he builds in this book on material learned in part from me, he tells the story in his own voice. And it is a voice that communicates interestingly and effectively to church officers and officer candidates—and hopefully beyond to many laymen—in today's Presbyterian churches, small or large.

It is important that responsible leaders in the church today have an understanding of the past history of the church. How could those of the Apostles' generation have provided the proper leadership of the church without knowledge of God's dealings with Abraham, Joseph, Moses, Samuel, David, and Daniel? So it continues to be the case as we seek to follow Paul's admonition to Timothy, *"What you have heard from me ... entrust to faithful men who will be able to teach others also"* (2 Timothy 2:2). This volume helps to carry out this mandate.

Will Barker
Birchwood, WI

## Preface

Since I have been waiting over thirty years to have the time and motivation to write this book, the purposes of writing have grown. Perhaps more importantly, the importance of having this kind of work—easy-to-read, dealing with basics—has grown even more.

As one of the fastest growing denominations in North America over the past three-plus decades, many people have begun attending and joined PCA churches knowing little if anything about what the denomination stands for and what its heritage really is. So I guess one of my primary purposes is to help readers come to these understandings.

I also believe this work is crucially important so that future leaders can better understand why the PCA is the way it is today (in 2005). We must learn from the mistakes made in our past heritage and in our own history, and not repeat them again. Because of this need, I also intend to write my own "Anecdotal History of the PCA" sometime in the next few years (God willing). I will call this book *Confessions of a Recovering T.R.* and give a personal, biographical history of those events and issues, which God has providentially placed in my path over the years. (By the way, I think all of us who were around in 1973 should do the same thing.—Wayne Sparkman at the PCA Historical Center agrees; he is waiting for your work!)

As the Presbyterian Church in America grows and thus moves further and further away from her beginnings in 1973 and the major Joining and Receiving event of 1982, it is very easy for people to loose touch with our roots. As I sit on the floor of Presbytery meetings and examine candidates for ordination, I am appalled at the consistent lack of appreciation many of these men have for their church's history. Even those that have studied the subject have a difficult time relating the facts they have learned to the reasons for the existence of the PCA.

I am firmly convinced that if members of the PCA do not obtain a solid understanding of our history—and I mean all members, not just teaching elders or even ruling elders and deacons—we will quickly lose our commitment to maintain the standards and principles for which many of our forefathers literally died. As I have pointed out in Chapter Sixteen on the division of the old PCA (Presbyterian Church *of* America) at their 3$^{rd}$ General Assembly in 1938, it was my understanding of the dynamics of this historical event that caused me to be committed to work for a compromise while serving as the Chairman of the Committee of Commissioners of the Mission to the World committee of the PCA (Presbyterian Church *in* America) at our 3$^{rd}$ General Assembly in 1975. I had great fear that history would repeat itself. We can—and should—learn from our history and it is my hope and prayer that this book may in some small way help others to learn from that history and thus help guide them and our church in the decades to come.

Another purpose of writing this kind of historical work is to help readers who are new to the theological underpinnings of the PCA—which are usually referred to as Reformed Theology, or Covenant Theology, and even sometimes as Calvinism—to come to a better understanding of that teaching. Some may ask what connection there is between understanding theology and learning a little church history. Let me tell you my story.

There was a time when I thought reading about and especially studying history was totally dry, boring and useless.

I will never forget the first day in the fall of 1973 in a Church History class when Dr. Will Barker began teaching for the first time at Covenant Seminary since he had been called as a Professor of Church History and Dean of the Faculty. As he went around the room that first day, he asked each of us to introduce ourselves briefly, especially telling a bit about their background and studies in the field of history.

When it came to my turn, I said (in a loud a firm voice as anyone who knows me would fully expect) something like this: "I have had three hours of Western Civ and three hours of History of the Old South and they were probably the two most useless classes I ever had as an undergrad!" With that pleasant, comforting smile that is invariably on Will's face, he said something like, "Well, Mr. Clements, I'll consider that a challenge to make this one of the most important classes you will have!" And, wouldn't you know it, I can honestly say it may have been exactly that—the most important class of my seminary education. It certainly was one of the two or three prime factors that led me to understand the Reformed faith.

This is not just my story—it is also my wife's story. She grew up in a conservative Southern Presbyterian church where her Dad was a long-time elder. She grew up believing the Bible was the word of God and that all of the fundamentals shared by evangelicals were true—but it was her exposure to church history that put it all into context and helped her understand the Reformed faith. During thirty-five years of ministry, I have heard that story repeated over and over again.

So God has at last provided me with the time and motivation to finish this work—and even though it started with class notes I took from Will Barker, and even though he should at least be the co-author of this work—I am thankful for his encouragement and advice in going ahead with the project.

Any of the good stuff you read, please attribute to Will—any of
the bad stuff is mine alone!

## *Acknowledgements*

To Dr. William S. Barker, my Church History Professor at Covenant Seminary in the 1970s—he "lit the fire" and I hope it never goes out.

To the adult Sunday school classes in a half dozen or more PCA churches—but most especially to the class at the Westminster Church in Roanoke, Virginia, who have been the kilns to refine much of the work by asking questions for which I had no answer on that particular day but was forced to look it up and include it in the finished work.

To Drs. Morton Smith and Charles Dunahoo who were willing to come to Roanoke to substitute for me in the Sunday School class during two weeks I was laid up following knee replacement surgery. Not only were they phenomenal substitute teachers, their lectures have become two of the significant chapters of this book and their encouragement to produce this work put me over the top at a point when my strength and motivation were waning.

To students in the field test of an on-line training course offered through Ruling Elder Training Academy (*www.rulingelder.com*) who worked through each chapter of this book as their text and themselves made suggestions on improving and clarifying portions—and then for their insights that went into developing Chapter Eighteen. Special thanks to Frank Root and Bob Mattes.

To the many who have asked over the past six to nine months "Is the history book done yet?" reinforcing what I have long sensed as a need.

To the young men in both New River and Blue Ridge Presbyteries over the past ten years who have demonstrated their woeful lack of knowledge and understanding of our denominational roots and have kept alive my intention to "git 'er done!"

To the growing number, who are asking when I will write the companion volume outlining the important details of the PCA's history during our first thirty-five years (it's on the list, fellows, but I'm not going to tell you how far down it is!)

To Joel Belz, founder of World Magazine (and an old, cherished friend), and Dr. Nick Willborn, Church History professor at Greenville Presbyterian Theological Seminary (and an enthusiastic new friend), who took time out of their busy schedules to read the manuscript and provide public recommendations as well as private encouragement.

Finally, to Mrs. Diane Hitzfeld, my editor, who constantly challenged me to fulfill my purpose to keep things as clear and concise as possible (which I probably failed to do in Chapter Seventeen, but it's so hard when you have been in the middle of the history about which you are writing!) She completed her work on this volume during limited spare time at nights and on weekends while helping the great cause of Desire Street Ministries as they rebuilt and restored the ministry following Hurricane Katrina's devastation, relocating the Academy to Baton Rouge, Louisiana in the fall of 2006.

Narrows, Virginia
February 2006

# Contents

# Chapter One
## The Church That Got Reformed

It is too simplistic to say that prior to the Protestant Reformation the Roman Catholic Church was corrupt and Luther revolted. We must also learn the details about the corruption, and how it spread and affected the events that took place during that period.

The political climate in the 15$^{th}$ Century was so different from ours in the early 21$^{st}$ Century that, even when we read the words, we have trouble contemplating what it was like. It was the end of the era of Middle-Age feudal society, where one strongman could control a large territory and keep it under his influence. It was becoming common for groups of these feudal lords to ban together to begin protecting a greater expanse of land. Many of these groupings were of peoples of similar ethnic heritage and the growth began what we now recognize as a "national state." Thus, the political climate was in flux and the art of "statesmanship" was just beginning.

The geographic and economic climates were intermingled and centered on Spain and Portugal, the two nations leading the way in global exploration. This resulted in a great expansion of trade and the influx of massive amounts of gold and silver brought back from the New World. As one would expect, those who became the "new rich" were far less committed to their more rural heritage, which inevitably resulted in the growth of cities where trade and business could be more easily conducted.

The world was undergoing its greatest changes in the areas of culture and intellectual interests. The 15$^{th}$ Century saw the growth of the Renaissance. One of the results was the advent of a movement known as Christian Humanism. Leaders of the movement taught the necessity of modern people to be concerned about morals—something that half a century earlier was much less emphasized. Another result was a growing interest in classical languages, especially Greek and Hebrew. Of course, this led to the reading of the older manuscripts of the Bible, initially just to better understand the language.

It will be my general policy throughout this book to focus more on the stories of people than on movements and theories. I firmly believe that the study of central historical figures is the best way for people today to understand history. People are what interests us most today, and it is in understanding people that we get the clearest picture of the Roman Catholic Church of this period, that is, the Church that got reformed.

Trying to find a starting place in a study of history is always difficult, but in this case, there is one person who stands head and shoulders above his peers over the course of several centuries and thus becomes the perfect person with whom to start. A priest known as Bernard of Clairvaux was certainly the greatest religious force of the 12$^{th}$ Century—if not for several centuries. He was born in France into a family of wealth; his dad was a knight. His mother was the strong religious influence on her son as she was, even more so than other mothers among her peers, deeply religious.

Bernard clearly had inherited his father's leadership skills. When he was twenty years old, he persuaded thirty of his friends to join a monastery with him. A few years later as a young priest, he was able to raise the needed resources to start his own monastery in the town of Clairvaux, France. His monastic life was the proper choice for Bernard. He wanted no part of the politics of a secular life, of which he was personally acquainted. He, like his mother, had developed a deep piety that—one can tell from his writings—was based on his own personal love for Jesus, so much so that two of the great Reformers that we will study soon, Luther and Calvin, both commented in their writings that they felt that Bernard was a "true evangelical."

Bernard was not only a man of prayer; he was also a man of action. He was a major player in the Roman Catholic Church of his era. One of his former students at the monastery in Clairvaux became Pope Eugene III and Bernard was able to exercise great influence. In fact, a close study of the Church in the 12$^{th}$ Century sees Bernard at the center of the solution of several major problems. From this involvement, he saw very early on the damage that was being done to the Church as it grew so quickly to great wealth, and most of his writings contain warnings on this specific problem.

Although they began in the late 11$^{th}$ Century, the series of planned invasions known as the Crusades carried on to the 13$^{th}$ Century and thus paralleled the time frame in which we are beginning our examination of the Church that got reformed. While the Muslim world of the time clearly had the greatest culture and trade of the age, the leaders of the Roman Catholic Church were focused on only one thing: to take back the Holy Land from the "infidels".

The Patriarch of Constantinople (the city in Turkey we now know as Istanbul) was the closest to the situation at the beginning and he contacted Pope Urban asking for help. After some consultation with other archbishops, the Pope decided that it was important for the Church to take the leadership in Europe and to use military force to "free" Jerusalem. Pope Urban began preaching the rationale for the First Crusade, and thus for the series of seven major war efforts, during the next 200 years.

Of the seven Crusades, only two could be considered successful in any way. The war was not won, but the most important outcome of the Crusades was not its effect in the Middle East of that day (although we may be feeling some serious effect of the Crusades in our day and age). The most important outcome was the growth of the power of the Papacy (a word regularly used to refer to the rule of Popes in the Church). The growth of the Papacy was symbolic of growth of Europe's status and power in the world.

Although earlier Popes were guilty of abusing the power of their office, we will focus on the best known and perhaps the most outrageous in the exercise of his power. As a young priest and even as a cardinal in the Church, Innocent III had been a man of personal humility and piety. Once he became Pope, however, he adopted an extremely high conception of the office and under him, it reached the very peak of power.

His power had effect in every major government in Europe. He held the power to dictate who would be heir to the German throne. When the King of France illegally divorced his wife, Innocent III stopped all religious services throughout the country until the King obeyed his edict and took his wife back. When King John of England did not want to appoint the Pope's choice for Archbishop of Canterbury (the highest ranking priest in the then totally Roman Catholic country), the Pope excommunicated the King! It would have been impossible to keep his throne without being Catholic, so he gave in to the Pope's pressure and made the appointment. (As an interesting

4

aside, this is the same King John, who was pressured by his people to sign the Magna Carta and began the process of developing democracy in the English-speaking world.)

Innocent III strongly centralized power within the Roman church hierarchy and actually made all decisions himself. The conquest of Constantinople during the Fourth Crusade even gave him power for a period of time over the Eastern Orthodox Church (which had divided from the Roman Church just over 150 years earlier). The Popes who came after Innocent III tried to maintain his power, but were unable to because they could not stand up to the level of his great leadership ability and his personal piety.

At the end of the 13$^{th}$ Century, a pope named Boniface VIII came to rule in Rome. He went beyond even Innocent III's views and practices. He saw himself as the ruler of all kings—all governments were to be in submission to the Church. He threatened to excommunicate any king who taxed Church property or priests. He declared that no one could possibly go to heaven unless he or she was a member of the Roman Catholic Church. He declared that all kings and worldly powers were subject to spiritual power, and that he, Pope Boniface VIII, represented that power on earth.

Finally, he came to a major showdown with King Philip of France over the arrest of a bishop. In order to exercise as much power as possible against the Pope, King Phillip called the first French States-General, a major meeting including clergy, nobility and common people. It was the first national assembly of its kind in Europe. The States-General upheld the action of the King and brought charges of heresy and immorality against the Pope. To create one of history's great cliffhangers, Philip had his troops kidnap the Pope just before he issued an order of excommunication against the King. The

Pope died just a month later, and the Papacy quickly went downhill from this point. Clearly, this conflict changed the swing of the pendulum and marked the important rise of nationalism versus the Papacy.

The Pope who followed Boniface lived less than a year. His successor was a Frenchman, who took the name of Clement V. Clement came from a wealthy family and was understandably spoiled; he pretty much got his way throughout all his life. Unlike Bernard, who also came from a family of wealth and stature, Clement developed grave moral faults, especially in the area sexual sins. Because of his spiritual weakness, he quickly fell under the power of King Philip who had developed a great deal power in his battle with Boniface.

The clearest illustration of King Philip's power was his demand that Clement move his offices from Rome to a town in southeastern France on the Rhone River, Avignon, in 1309. Understand that every nation or large people group had its own archbishop, and the archbishop of Rome had become the "leading" archbishop and ultimately the Pope of the entire Church. For the Pope to move out of Rome, meant that the archbishop of Italy had moved to France!

This move solidified King Philip's power over the Roman Catholic Church. For the next seventy years, all Popes were Frenchmen. Each of them was under the total domination and political power of the King of France. The government heavily taxed churches, as well as the people through their church, to support the civil government. Anyone desiring to be a priest, a bishop, or any other kind of church official had to pay the equivalent of one year's wages to the civil government. Because of the seventy year period of his situation (paralleling the seventy years that Israel was in captivity in Babylon), this period of history is know as the Babylonian Captivity of the Papacy. It lasted until 1377.

As if this situation weren't bad enough, ultimately a total schism came in the Papacy. One French Pope (named Gregory XI), during a period of several political upheavals in France and Italy, decided to move the headquarters back to Rome. He died shortly after the move. The people of Rome demonstrated in vast numbers, and demanded that the Papacy stay in Rome; they physically threatened harm to the cardinals who were gathered there for the election of the new Pope. Demonstrating not one whit of backbone, the Cardinals quickly elected an Italian as the new Pope. Trouble was, in the haste of the election, they picked a scoundrel who everyone— French, Italian, whoever—very soon wanted to get rid of.

Four months later, the very same Cardinals gathered and, breaking centuries of precedence, voted to declare their first choice void since it had been dictated by mob violence. They then quickly voted a Frenchman as the new Pope. This not only failed to solve the problem, it created an even greater problem. Now there were *two* Popes, both elected by the same College of Cardinals. The Italian Pope was acknowledged by the people of Italy, Germany, Scandinavia and England. The French Pope was acknowledged in France, Spain, Scotland, Sicily and part of Germany—an approximately equal number of supporters for each one.

Getting rid of this new problem was not easy. Cardinals on both sides agreed that something had to be done, so they decided to call a meeting with representatives from both the French and Italian camps. After much difficulty and political maneuvering, a "Council" (as these church meetings had been called historically) was held in the Northern Italian town of Pisa in 1409. Neither Pope was present; they both denied the right of the Council even to meet.

The Council did not deal with the tough issues of needed reform in the Church. All they were able to accomplish was to find a compromise candidate…and they elected him Pope! Now there were *three* Popes—Italian, French, and the Council's Pope!

Finally, into this void of power stepped a man with great leadership and vision, a secular leader, a fellow named Sigismund. He was the King of Hungary and of Bohemia and ultimately became the Emperor of the Holy Roman Empire. His plan also was to call a Council to meet on the issue, but to ensure that everyone's interests were represented.

The Council was held in the town of Constance, located on a lake that borders on the area that we know today as West Germany, Austria and Switzerland. The Council of Constance was the most brilliant and largely attended gathering of the entire Middle Ages. More people than cardinals attended. All kinds of leaders—Church, government, business, and laity— were there.

After carefully examining the issues, the Council exerted its authority over all in the Church, including all three competing Popes. It deposed the current Conciliary Pisan Pope, who was named John XXIII. (His title was picked up a couple of decades ago by a real Roman Pope.) He, too, had used his power for his own benefit and had become totally corrupt and immoral.

The Italian Pope, utilizing some quick judgment, voluntarily resigned his position. The Council at length convinced several of the nations that were part of the coalition supporting the French Pope (Spain and Scotland) to withdraw their support, and he was finally deposed. In 1417, three years after the Council of Constance started, it elected one new Pope. He was a Roman cardinal, and thus demonstrated that the German and Italian leaders had finally subdued French power. This marked the beginning of the Renaissance Papacy.

This series of continuing fiascos concerning the Popes was terrible, but the corruption did not exist only at the top. Not only did the popes become degenerate, but corruption was also rampant throughout the clergy. Very few priests could read. Most of them were not answering a spiritual call, but rather had purchased the rights to their office, thinking it to be a pleasant lifestyle. On top of their personal degeneration, they would even resort to religious practices far from those promoted by the Church—they practiced witchcraft and devil worship. During this period, a series of plagues spread through Europe that brought on great spiritual depression among the people. Their priests were not equipped to deal with the problems.

We learn from biblical principle that when the church has weak and evil leaders, the entire church is affected. Thus, with bad priests, the result was bad people, and the evil was even deeper among the people.

As horrible as all this sounds, we must not think that everyone in the Roman Catholic Church was bad. We must remember this was still the true Church of Jesus Christ, and God always promises to keep a remnant of true believers. Among this remnant, a few men stand out as "pre-Reformers."

To find the first of these, we have to look as far back as 300 years before the Reformation. In the French city of Lyons, lived a leading, wealthy merchant named Peter Waldo. Well after he had amassed his fortune, around the age of forty, Peter underwent a conversion experience. While mourning the death of a close friend, Waldo began to read the Bible. At about the same time, he heard a traveling minstrel singing a religious song. Peter was led to speak to a priest about the major spiritual change in his life.

Peter Waldo visited his parish priest, who for whatever motivation (knowing that his parishioner was one of the wealthiest men in the area), counseled him with the words of Matthew 19:21. *"Jesus said to him, 'If you would be perfect, go, sell what you possess and give to the poor, and you will have treasure in heaven; and come, follow me.'"* Inexplicably, Waldo took the advice literally. He gave his wife and children a trust fund on which to live. He repaid all the prior interest he had earned in business and he sold everything else he had (which was still a bunch) and gave it directly to the poor of the city.

Peter then left town and started a life as an itinerant preacher. Since he had no money left, he had to live as a beggar. His old friends disowned him, some believing he had lost his mind. But he quickly made many new friends. Many of the poor people of Lyons, who had benefited from his gratitude to them, became his traveling companions and even started to preach with Waldo. Although they were very hard to find (since Rome did not want their parishioners to read the Scriptures— that was the responsibility of the priest—if he could read!), Waldo was able to obtain copies of parts of the Bible translated into French, mostly the Gospels.

Very quickly, Waldo became well known in the region. Thus, he came to the attention of the local bishop. Being confronted with a layperson, who was preaching and distributing copies of the Bible translated into the local language (both of which were outlawed by Rome), he banned him from the diocese. Peter and his band took to the mountains where his preaching among the small towns and rural regions became even more famous. Ultimately, this situation came to the attention of the Pope.

Waldo was summoned to a council meeting before the Pope himself to answer charges. In a mixed verdict, the Pope approved the group's vows of poverty but said they could not preach any more. Returning to France, Peter and his followers decided they must follow God and not man, and resumed their itinerant preaching of the Bible. However, they worked hard to stay out of the scrutiny of the Church, so not much is known about Waldo after that. One later Pope did find the group to be heretics, *in absentia*.

There were signs of the growth of groups of Christians who identified themselves as Waldensians, especially in the mountain area of Northern Italy. There are even a handful of small churches yet today in New York City and in rural North Carolina who identify themselves as Waldensians. Whatever his true history turned out to be, one thing is for sure: Peter Waldo was the very first of the pre-Reformation reformers in the Roman Catholic Church.

The next early Reformer worthy of note is John Wycliffe. He lived about 150 years before the Reformation. He was a teacher and scholar in England who had been greatly influenced by the realism of St. Augustine's writings (which was very different from the reigning philosophy of his day and age). Like so many others in the Church at that time, Wycliffe became a priest through his political connections rather than through his spiritual calling to the office.

Once in the Church, Wycliffe became aware of the depth of corruption within the Church and began speaking out, especially in the area of wealth. He was teaching at Oxford at the time and began publicly teaching on the problems in the Church. His antidote was to require vows of poverty. Needless to say, the "higher-ups" in the clergy didn't much care for Wycliffe and his views. The Bishop of London summoned him to his office and ordered him to stop teaching those views, but he was not punished because of his great public popularity throughout England.

Wycliffe then began to write pamphlets expressing his views, to which he added his view (learned from Augustine's writings) that the Bible must be the ultimate authority in the Church, rather than the Pope's. He went so far as to write that any Pope who grasped worldly power and was eager for taxes is by presumption not among God's elect and therefore is the Antichrist. The more he read of the Bible, the more he became opposed to the traditional Papacy.

Wycliffe next became convinced that the common people in England should be able to read the Bible themselves in their native tongue. As in the rest of the world, the Bible was generally only available in Latin. Only priests (or at least some of the priests) were able to read Latin. Wycliffe himself translated the New Testament into English, and as you would expect, it was widely received and appreciated throughout the country. He also recruited a group of disciples, known as "poor priests" although none of them were actually recognized priests, who went throughout the country, living under vows of poverty. This vow required them to beg for sustenance, to walk barefoot, clad in long robes with staffs in their hands, wandering two-by-two, preaching the gospel. They become know as Lollards (a pejorative name given the group, as the root meaning of the word is "to mutter").

The institutional church waited until they knew Wycliffe was near death before officially declaring him a heretic. When Wycliffe died of natural causes in his own parish, most of his followers were forced to flee to Europe. They settled in a section that was then called Bohemia; it is the area we now know as the Czech Republic. Their descendents would become major players in the Reformation that would follow more than 100 years later.

The next important early Reformer was Jan Hus. He lived about 100 years before the Reformation. Hus was born in the area of Bohemia and may well have been influenced by followers of Wycliffe, although we have little historical proof. Hus completed college and immediately went into the priesthood. He was never as radical as Wycliffe had been, but certainly followed the same heritage. Hus became the rector of a great university during the period when Bohemia became a powerful, independent country. From this position, he began to advocate the authority of Scripture over Popes and Councils, as well as the preaching of the Word of God to all the people.

Through an interesting providence of God (there are no real coincidences in God's work, are there?), the Council of Constance (the one that finally solved the three-Pope crisis) dealt with Wycliffe's heresy at the same time. They decided that Wycliffe's teaching was so terrible that they had his body exhumed from its grave and then burned as a sign of their judgment that he was in Hell. Then, they sent for Hus!

Being a fairly wise person, Hus understood what was going to happen...but he went to meet with the Council anyway. There, under severe questioning, he held to his principles, knowing that if he recanted he would be safe. Nevertheless, Hus proclaimed that the Word of God was of higher authority than the word of the Council, and he was condemned and burned at the stake. As early as 100 years before the Reformation, people were already dying in defense of the concept that would become known as *Sola Scriptura* (the

Scriptures alone)—one of the great Reformation principles still followed today.

There is one other significant event also worth looking at; it started at about the same time as Hus lived. Beginning with the Council of Pisa (the one begun to figure out what to do with the two-Pope crisis) and continuing with the Council of Constance, a movement developed—known as the Conciliary Movement—to continue to advocate removing power away from one man or a small group of men and give it to a representative body of the people. While its origins were within a religious context, the principles were transferable to the sphere of government.

A scholar named Marsiglio of Padua (who is not well known in secular history) began to write extensively on this subject. He was a student of Aristotle and learned in his studies that power should be vested in the people. That is, the people should decide who should rule over them, and this should be true in both the State and the Church. (This, of course, became one of the foundational principles of Presbyterian Church Government!) Marsiglio went so far as to deny the supremacy of Peter among the Apostles (which was a central tenant in the Roman Catholic teaching leading to the establishment of the Papacy).

While this was a philosophical position of tremendous potential, Marcella lacked any real zeal or personal leadership, so few followed him. This movement was successful in solving the crisis in the Papacy, but it also sought to stifle all teaching that was contrary to current Church traditions. As you can already sense, the Roman Catholic Church at the beginning of the 16th Century was ripe for being known historically as the Church that got reformed.

## Chapter Two
## *What Was the Protestant Reformation?*

Like so many other things in the study of history, the further we get away from the Protestant Reformation, the more we lose touch with what really happened. We also find that more wrong answers to our question, "What was the Protestant Reformation?" are put forward as factual. Let's begin by looking at some of those wrong answers.

Some have said the Reformation was a simple political revolution—an uprising resulting in the overthrow of authority and government. You know, like Lenin in Russia, or Mao in China, or Fidel in Cuba. While there were political changes taking place at the same time as the Reformation was occurring (we'll look at those shortly), they certainly were not that simple, or even closely identified as the same thing.

Others—particularly those who would identify themselves as political liberals—would propose an answer that this was a backward step of the advance of society. However, this merely superimposes their ideas that any advance requires the loosening of religious beliefs and practices. There was still much "renaissance growth" taking place during the time of the Reformation.

Another wrong answer is that the Reformation was a victory of the middle class—the bourgeois—over the lower classes. Yes, during this period, there was some development of a middle class in portions of Europe, but it is impossible to draw causal connections to religious changes. Many of those who were followers of the leaders of the Reformation were in fact poor people. We saw that in the previous lesson with the poor people of Lyons following Waldo and the Lollards following Wycliffe.

Modern day libertarians will claim that the Reformation was simply the beginning of the growth of individual liberties. I have some sympathy with that assertion, for certainly one of the hallmarks of the Reformation was the priesthood of all believers (a topic we will study a bit later). But this is still too simplistic. Much, much more was happening in the Church that got reformed.

Well, what then are the right answers to our question, "What was the Protestant Reformation?" I believe the right answers can be summarized under four headings. It was first and foremost a revival in the Church. It was secondarily, but importantly, a full-blown revolution in civilization (rather than a simple political overthrow of governments). Thirdly, it was most clearly a work of God. Finally, for our purposes in this study seeking to focus on people rather than theories, it was the work of a tremendous hero (plus some others, who were heroes as well).

First, let's see how the Reformation can be looked at in terms of revival. To see this we need to understand the biblical pattern for revival. Be careful not to superimpose what has become the pattern of manmade or human-led revivals of recent history. In biblical revival, you always find the same elements. The people of God—the established church—reaches a low point in their existence. There are fewer and fewer godly people left who both believe in God and follow his path for their life. Into this type of crisis, God will always raise up from the remnant of true believers a great leader, and through the work of that leader bring about a revival of true religion. I think the name of a few biblical characters will help make this point: Moses, Joshua, the good judges, David, Elijah, the Apostles at Pentecost. I think you can see the point.

Now, at the time of the Reformation, there were three very important issues at stake and by understanding these issues we can see how low a mark had been reached in the true Church. The issues are: grace alone, the Scriptures alone and the priesthood of believers.

The first of these came to be known by its Latin name— *Sola Gratia*). The issue was the very means of salvation. Did salvation come to man as a gracious gift from God—by grace alone—or did salvation come as the result of some effort, some work, on the part of man. This issue had been settled nearly 1,000 years earlier in the Church—at the time of Augustine when the church declared Pelagius a heretic. At the time of the Reformation, however, that truth had once again been called into question. So much so, that in his book *The Bondage of the Will*, Luther said salvation by grace was the key issue of his day.

Sometimes this same theological truth goes by the name *Sole Fide*—by faith alone. It's not really a different issue, just a different aspect of the same issue. Faith is indeed the operative function by which a person trusts in Jesus, and that faith is, itself, a gift that comes from God. That gift of faith is given by grace alone.

The second issue also is known historically by its Latin title: *Sola Scriptura*—by the Scriptures alone. At the time of the Reformation, the Roman Catholic Church recognized three sources of authority: the Bible, the traditions of the Church and the edicts of the Pope. All three of these were held as having authority in what the Church believed, taught and practiced.

But Luther and the other heroes of the Reformation all came to the conclusion—that they learned as they carefully read their Bibles—that the only source of truth and authority for believers, and therefore for the Church, comes from the Bible alone. It was the very concept for which Wycliffe and Hus were condemned. It was the very concept for which Luther (whom we'll discuss later) was put on trial.

While evangelical churches today hold fast to the tenets of *Sola Gratia* (or *Sola Fide*), the *Sola Scriptura* issue is once again in trouble—oh, not from the traditions of the Church or the edicts of the Pope. But rather, from an ever-growing movement that says we receive truth both from the Bible and from new, direct revelation from God. We'll talk more about this a bit later.

The third major issue of the Reformation was known as the priesthood of all believers. At the time of Luther, it was the common teaching of the Roman Catholic Church that individual believers had to come to the Church for mediation with God. Only through receiving the seven Sacraments of the Church could they be assured of the forgiveness of sins—and they were by this time even adding other "special" forms of mediation to those seven.

The idea of a priesthood of believers is still believed held in Protestant circles today, but in some cases, it is practiced out of context. Some take this concept to the extreme saying that since the individual has personal access to the throne of grace, there is no need at all for the Church. "I can function quite well as a solitary Christian, thank you very much." You will see in this study that this was never the belief, or the teaching, or the practice of any of the Reformers. All were high churchmen— they were just no longer Roman Catholic churchmen.

# What Was the Protestant Reformation?

In summary, I think we can safely say that the Protestant Reformation was the greatest back-to-the-Bible movement, yes even the greatest revival, since the time of Jesus.

Now to our second correct answer to the question of the day—"What was the Protestant Reformation?" It was, in a very real sense, a revolution in civilization. It was not just a simple political revolution where one group takes over the government from another group. It was much deeper, much more significant than just that. But let me be clear about this—this is simply a secondary outworking of the Reformation. It was never the purpose of any of the Reformers. It was never a direct achievement of the work of the Reformers. It was simply the result of what happens when people go back to the Bible—and read it, and believe it, and start acting in accordance with the teaching of it.

These "revolutionary" secondary results took place in various areas of life. One was the growth of a movement that became known as nationalism. This was especially true in Germany, but you begin to see the same thing in the Netherlands, Scotland and even England. People began functioning in larger political identities—going beyond the city-state concepts or strongman leadership concepts of the Middle Ages.

The second area of life in which we see these revolutionary results is the growth of constitutional democracies. This happened quickly in Switzerland, and then spread to England and the Netherlands. They were much slower in coming to the rest of Europe—but ultimately they came.

The third area was that of economics. All of a sudden it was OK for someone to be a strong believer in Jesus—a practicing Christian—and work at secular jobs. In the past, if you wanted to be a practicing Christian, you joined a monastery or became a priest. Now, the common man, upon learning the good news of the gospel and trusting in Jesus alone for the assurance of salvation, would remain in his secular calling. And when people started putting biblical principles to work in the secular world, the economic structure began to radically change.

The same thing was true in the area of family life. All of a sudden, it was OK for a Christian to be married and raise children, even those in leadership roles as ministers—preachers and teachers. The next thing you knew, all people who were learning to follow Jesus began applying those principles to their own family lives. In many ways, this may have been the most thorough revolution of civilization.

Any one of these facets of the effects of the Reformation on civilization could fill the pages of a book—and this is so very true of the final area; that of education. Just think about the impact. The Reformers wanted the people to learn the Bible and knew they had to read it for themselves. Then here comes a guy named Gutenberg, just two generations earlier, and he invents a printing press.

All of a sudden, it was easy to get copies of the Scriptures into the hands of the people and they were motivated to learn to read. The guys who owned the printing presses wanted to make more money—so they began printing other great books and people would read them. Education would never be the same again. Talk about revolutionary change!

Now we want to move to the next (which is the third) correct answer to our question of the day—"What was the Protestant Reformation?" We probably should have started with this answer, because it was, after all, the work of God. We need to recall some important theological truths with which I will assume we are all aware. God is sovereign over his creation—but this sovereignty does not mean that he works apart from the circumstances of life and history. God sends rain. And the result of rain can be both good and bad. It's good when trees and plants grow and produce oxygen so humans and animals can breathe. Our Church's Confession of Faith speaks to this in the Chapter of Providence, when it says (I'm paraphrasing just a little to make it come out in 21$^{st}$ Century English), "God, in His ordinary providence, makes use of means (of circumstances), yet is free to work without these means, and above these means, and against these means, in His own pleasure." (WCF V-4). In the case of the Reformation, he did all of the above, but primarily, he worked through circumstances—and it is these circumstances we will be covering throughout this series.

We want to also understand the work of God in relation to the biblical concept of "the fullness of time." This concept comes to us from the pen of the Apostle Paul, as he writes in Galatians 4:4, *"But when the fullness of time had come, God sent forth his Son..."* Paul understood that God acts when things are right for acting. There is no doubt that things were right for acting at the time of the Reformation. While it could apply to any number of different events of that time, the printing press itself is proof that the "fullness of time" was ripe for a back-to-the-Bible revival.

Likewise, we understand that God is "outside" history—he is transcendent, as the theologians like to say. He exceeds, he lies beyond the limits of ordinary experience. Yet at the same time, he acts in history. He is not a clockmaker that designs this very wonderful clock, winds it up, puts it on a shelf (or axis, if you will) and watches it run. He tinkers with it—all the time— making it better, fixing it when necessary. It is in this way that God was acting in the time of the Reformation.

As is most often the case, God acts through people of his choosing. And so the fourth answer—and the most complete and at the same time the most complex answer to our question of the day, "What was the Protestant Reformation?" is this: it was the work of a tremendous hero (plus others).

## Chapter Three
## Heroes of the Reformation

Recently I did an internet search on favorite superheroes. While the search was not scientific, I came to what I believe is a reasonable conclusion. As of today, the two favorite superheroes are clearly Superman and Batman, and they are just about 50/50 as to who is the top of the various lists. Spiderman comes in a close third—but I think that's a result of the recent movies.

When we look at the Reformation, we have a number of heroes to look at. Here, the voting has been in for nearly five centuries, and the winner is clear—hands down—without a doubt: Martin Luther.

In this chapter, we want to give the fourth and (from my perspective for learning the historical roots of the Presbyterian Church in America) most important answer to our question from the previous chapter, "What was the Protestant Reformation?" That fourth answer is it was the work of a tremendous hero (plus many others). That tremendous hero, that superhero who was used by God to bring to pass the revival we call the Protestant Reformation, was indeed Martin Luther.

As far as I am concerned, dates are not all that important to learn in the study of history, as long as you can place the person in the correct century, and, if possible, in the correct part of that century. Luther, who was born in 1483 and died in 1546, was placed in the first half of the 16th Century.

While his entire life is important and worth studying, there was a three and one-half year period, during which the events of most intensity took place, starting with the posting of his 95 Theses in 1517 and ending at the Diet of Worms (pronounced "verms") in 1521. Before looking at these events, we must learn at least something of Luther's background.

As we examine the history of the early life and education of Martin Luther, we are immediately confronted with what is a very unique problem in the study of history. That is that we have *too much* information about those years, and thus it is difficult to separate fact from fiction.

Needless to say, the reporting and interpreting of the history surrounding Luther is highly influenced by whether or not one appreciates his work. Reading his early history from, say, a conservative, traditional Roman Catholic web site today, one would believe that he was an abused child who developed deep psychotic problems and a resulting personality that could not stand to be under authority.

Reading his early history from, say a traditional Lutheran web site today one would believe that he was the most brilliant, and at the same time, most holy, godly man to live in the 16th Century. The truth is somewhere in-between, but, from my own personal perspective, leans towards the brilliant/godly side.

Luther was raised in a rural, copper mining area of Germany, just into the old East Germany area of Saxony-Anhalt, in the southern half of the country. The town is named Eisleben, about thirty miles west of the major city of Leipzig.

His family was originally of the peasant class, but his father became successful through his mining interest, although he never became wealthy. He did have enough money, however, to provide a solid education for his son, Martin. The father's dream was that Martin would go to law school so he sent him first to a Cathedral school that was operated by a very Roman Catholic group known as The Brethren of the Common Life. They emphasized not only solid education, but also sought to instill a deep love for God—we would call them Pietists today.

At the age of eighteen, Luther entered the university and received a degree in philosophy two years later. He went on to graduate school and complete his master's degrees with honors by the age of twenty-two, and was preparing to go to law school. In 1505, a life-changing event took place that Luther himself referred to as "the thunderstorm event." During his examinations for his Master's degree, a close friend was killed in an accident. Several weeks, later while walking in a rainstorm, Luther was nearly struck by a bolt of lightning that came to earth very close to him.

Like nearly every Christian of those days (especially those trained in pietistic schools), he felt there was no escape from Hell, except through the Church and her Sacraments, pilgrimages, indulgences and the like. Assurance was a foreign idea to such folks. In the midst of dealing with his grief at the death of a close friend, as well as his own near-death experience, Luther was just plain scared.

One biography relates that, at the moment the lightening struck, he exclaimed "St. Anne, help me. I shall become a monk!" This was a clear demonstration of his trust and belief in the system, then widely believed, that saints would intercede on behalf of a poor, desperate soul.

Whatever he might have said, his actions proved what was in his heart. He not only turned to the Church, he turned to the Church "whole hog" as we say in Virginia. He became a monk, entering the Augustinian monastery at nearby Erfurt. And, as monks of those days would do, he dropped out of all secular, worldly pursuits.

In the monastery, Luther devoted himself to prayer, singing, study and meditation. He did so well that in less than two years, his supervisor selected him to become a priest. Even this did not give him peace with God. As he was saying his first mass, he had another crisis.

During the mass, he found himself reciting the words, "We offer unto thee, the living, the true, the eternal God..." As he later told the story, "At these words I was utterly stupefied and terror-stricken. I thought to myself, 'Who am I, that I should lift up my eyes or raise my hands to the divine Majesty? The angels surround him. At his nod the earth trembles. And shall I—a miserable little pygmy—say, "I want this, I ask for that?" For I am dust and ashes and full of sin and I am speaking to the living, eternal and true God."' The young priest was shaken. It took every ounce of his power just to stay at the altar long enough to finish saying the mass.

After that, Luther worked even harder to earn God's approval. He prayed even more than the rules of the monastery required. He studied theology for long hours; he got his degree as a Doctor of Theology. He fasted, sometimes going three days in a row without eating a crumb. He went to confession constantly, in accordance with his Church's teaching that, in order for sins to be forgiven, they must be confessed to a priest. He knew that there had to be some sins he was overlooking. If his salvation depended on his ability to recall every last sin and confess it to the priest, then he was surely lost.

He kept searching for peace. It frightened him to think of God, so he thought of God's Son, Jesus. He knew that Jesus would return to judge the world, and that frightened him all the more. He turned his prayers to Jesus' mother, Mary; he hoped she might be tender and compassionate and put in a good word for him. It didn't help.

He chose twenty-one dead saints as his special patrons, three for each day of the week, and he prayed to them. Even that didn't help. There he was—a priest, a theologian, a monk—completed devoted to the practice of religion—and yet no matter what he tried, it couldn't put him in a right relationship with God.

Within a year of his ordination, he was assigned to teach philosophy at the University of Wittenberg. At first, he did not teach the Bible or theology, but only philosophy—until he completed his Doctorate in 1512. Shortly before receiving the degree, he made his first trip to Rome (as was the custom with men being raised to that level of teaching in the Church). During the trip, he saw for himself—really for the first time anywhere—the level of corruption among the clergy and other Church leaders (as we discussed in the chapter on "The Church That Got Reformed"). He felt that the masses he attended were simply routine events following a timed schedule and totally lacking in worship. At one point, he fell on the steps of the Basilica in an expression of both prayer and deep frustration.

- After taking up his teaching duties the following year, he was assigned to teach several significant books of the Bible. The first was the Psalms, which he taught throughout 1513 and 1514. For the next two years, he taught Romans. During one of these years—and biographers are not unified on exactly which—the famous "tower experience" took place. (He did his study in a room in the tower of the university cathedral.) I will recount the story as told by those who hold to the timeframe in which he was teaching Romans.

As Luther was preparing to teach a class on Romans, he kept coming across a phrase that puzzled him. It was the phrase "the righteousness of God." This phrase appears four times in the first three chapters of Romans. He took the phrase to mean that God is righteous and acts righteously by punishing those who are wicked. That was a terrifying thought. Luther wrote, "My situation was that, although an impeccable monk, I stood before God as a sinner troubled in conscience, and I had no confidence that my merit could assuage him. Therefore I did not love a just and angry God, but rather hated and murmured against him... ...Night and day I pondered until I saw the connection between the righteousness of God and that statement (also in Romans) that "the righteous shall live by his faith."

"Then I grasped that the righteousness of God is the righteousness by which, through grace and sheer mercy, God justified us through faith. I felt myself to be reborn and to have gone through open doors into paradise. The whole of Scripture took on a new meaning. This passage became to me a gate to heaven."

28

It is clear that this experience was—in a real sense— the real beginning of the Protestant Reformation. It began with the first tenet—*Sola Fide* (by faith alone). Today we call it Justification by Faith.

However, while the Reformation started in a small room in a tower, it took effect far beyond that room. At a time most likely after the tower experience (again, biographers are vague on some of these dates), Luther was assigned to be the preacher of the Castle Church in Wittenberg. Much of the congregation was students, but included non-university-related folks as well.

Everyone agrees that Luther's preaching was strong, and straight from the Bible. The people were not used to this kind of preaching. In what was a shock to folks of that time, but makes perfectly good sense to us today, the congregation quickly began to grow—even to the point of overflowing the sanctuary on a regular basis.

Soon Luther was preaching about major issues facing the Church of his day (this came to a head in the 1516-1517 time frame). One such issue was Nominalism, a philosophical position from men like William of Ockham. Another issue was the church's use of indulgences. We must pause at this point to be sure we understand this issue.

During the Crusades, in an effort to raise funds for the armies, the Roman Catholic Church had begun to sell instruments that promised the buyer an exemption from religious acts. It was a basic teaching of the Church that one had to perform acts of penance—essentially going to confession with a priest, confessing sin, and being instructed by the priest to perform acts of penance as a way to express one's sorrow for the sin, thus receiving forgiveness.

When I grew up in the Catholic Church in the 1940s, I recall having to leave the confessional and going to a pew with a rosary and saying a certain number of memorized short prayers—usually going by the title "Hail, Mary's" or "Our Father's."

Needless to say, if one wanted to keep short accounts with God, knowing that any sins that had not been absolved by a priest and contingent upon doing penance, then one had to spend a lot of time at Church. These indulgences were ways to shortcut this process.

Based on some major religious act—such as a pilgrimage to a shrine—or even better, by a financial contribution to the work of the Church—one could receive an indulgence that allowed him to be exempt from these frequent acts of penance.

At first, the practice was workable—and most people still understood their need to confess and repent of sins. It wasn't long, however, before some naturally gifted salesmen—who also just happened to be priests—crossed the line. They would offer the indulgences as some sort of magic piece of paper. Some would go so far as to say that it didn't even matter if you had true confession and repentance in your heart, the indulgence would keep you in a right relationship with God all by itself.

Luther attacked this scurrilous practice regularly from the pulpit. However, in the year 1517, things reached the boiling point. Parallel with the time of Luther's attacks from the pulpit, a monk of the Dominican order named John Tetzel was traveling around the area of Germany where Luther served and was selling indulgences. These particular indulgences were based on gifts to be used to finish the building of the great St. Peter's Basilica in Rome—the one you see all the time in TV pictures today.

Anyway, in an effort to win the award for "salesman of the year" (so to speak), Tetzel would tell folks that these indulgences were so special that not only could it help the giver individually, they could help friends and loved ones who had previously died and were spending long years, perhaps centuries, in Purgatory as penance for unconfessed sin. This practice had become absolutely ridiculous, evidenced by the fact that Tetzel had made up a slogan for his sales campaign—perhaps as a forerunner to the Madison Avenue of today—"As soon as the coin in the coffer rings, the soul from purgatory springs!"

Needless to say, Luther felt that what Tetzel was doing was not just bad theology, it was downright ungodly. This was the proverbial straw that broke the camel's back. Luther prepared 95 different propositions (which were referred to as theses in those days) dealing with many of the problems he saw in the Roman Catholic Church, but mostly highlighting those surrounding the issue of indulgences.

As was the practice in those days, both students and teachers would go up to the door of the Castle Church and pin up papers with their theses as a way to broaden the discussion of topics. The church door was their internet blog. While things didn't travel quite as fast then as they do in our day and age, with amazing speed those 95 theses spread throughout all of Germany, and the Dominican brothers of Tetzel denounced Luther—who was an Augustinian monk, you may recall—as a man of "dangerous doctrines." The debate raged in every theological circle in the land. It did not take long for the issue to come to the attention of the Pope and, in 1518, Luther was called to Rome for heresy proceedings, which could, in those days, result in death. It was at this time, however, the civil government in Germany stepped into the picture.

While there was in fact a confederation known as the Holy Roman Empire in place in Germany, and Charles V was the newly installed incumbent at that time, real power was still held by local leaders. In the area of Germany where Luther lived and taught, that local leader was known as Frederick the Elector, the prince of Saxony. While Charles V, as well as his predecessor, Maximillian, had both publicly announced their disapproval of Luther's views, Frederick was sympathetic and held enough sway that he was able to convince Rome to hold the trial in Germany—thus protecting Luther's very life.

The Pope sent one of his cardinals with the full authority to take any necessary steps of discipline. Cardinal Cajetan, one of the Pope's most trusted advisors (and who was from the same Dominican order as Tetzel) surprisingly declared Luther's teachings out of accord with the Church and insisted Luther stop teaching them, but did not excommunicate him. The details of all these decisions are most interesting, but spelling them out is beyond the purpose of an introductory book such as this.

About this time, another priest named Philip Melanchthon joined Luther on the faculty at Wittenberg, and also joined him in teaching the truth of justification by faith alone. Melanchthon turned out to be a more skilled theologian than Luther, but did not have the strong personality and leadership skills of Luther. Actually, they made a great team. Melanchthon is a very important figure in Lutheran history.

As Luther would continue to debate his critics in the Church throughout Germany, in 1519 he entered into one debate that lasted for eighteen days in the nearby city of Leipzig with the resident theologian there, named John Eck. At one point in this debate, Luther began to question the church's very authority, crying out, "A council may sometimes err. Neither the Church nor the Pope can establish articles of faith. These must come from the Scripture." It was from this point that the second major tenant of the Reformation began to take form—*Sola Scriptura*, the Scriptures alone.

Luther then began to write many pamphlets, printed sermons and other documents and made sure they were distributed throughout Germany and even throughout Europe. This was probably the reason the Reformation spread so rapidly. He ran a great "campaign."

Of these documents, three stand out. One was a direct attack on the authority of the Pope. The second was an attack on the number and necessity of the Sacraments of the Church. (As you are probably aware, the Roman Catholic Church recognizes seven Sacraments, while Protestants recognize only the two of Baptism and the Lord's Supper.) And the third entitled, "Freedom of the Christian Man," set forth the necessity of faith in order to be right with God.

One lesson we can learn as modern day Presbyterians is that it is important to get good, accessible biblical materials into the hands of the people—which is part of my purpose in developing the current series of Presbyterian primers.

Luther's campaign just heated things up all the more and Rome sent another Cardinal and gave Luther a document known as a Papal Bull. It was a formal letter of discipline, telling him to renounce his position or he would be excommunicated. This Papal Bull was even more serious than the previous pronouncement, yet Luther burned it publicly in the square in Wittenberg before a large crowd of cheering onlookers. There was no turning back now.

This was heady stuff. It was not just a couple of pinheads debating in a small classroom—the entire country was involved. (Think "O.J. trial"!)

The next step was for the Pope to have the emperor hand Luther over to the Church to be brought back to Rome for a trial, which would obviously result in punishment by death for heresy. The young emperor, Charles V, was unable to wield enough civil power to bring that about, so in January 1521, Pope Leo X declared Luther a heretic and pronounced that he was expelled from the Church. As you might expect, that didn't slow him down for an instant.

Emperor Charles V then decided to call a meeting, known in those days as a "Diet," to call Luther to account. In German history, the Diet originated as a meeting of landholders, sometimes called "burghers," and they would be called together by the local ruler to discuss financial problems. After the formation of the Holy Roman Empire, the Diet became a loose assembly of both Church and civil leaders. Charles V called a meeting of the Diet to be held in the city of Worms. Luther's protector, Frederick of Saxony, provided guards to travel with him, and they made the trip much like a political campaign—stopping each night in a different city and conducting public meetings. They didn't take the short route—they made sure they stopped at the largest cities in the area—even Frankfurt. Finally, they arrived, and Luther appeared before the Diet.

The events of his examination are great drama and I encourage all to read about it—or at least see the movie! After hours of questioning, Luther was given one last chance to recant and spent a night in prayer. The next day he returned and made his now famous statement— reiterating his growing stand on *Sola Scriptura.* "My conscience is captive to the Word of God. I will not recant anything, for to go against conscience is neither honest nor safe. Here I stand. I cannot do otherwise. God help me."

There were immediate political attempts to continue to find compromise, but Luther would not give in. Finally, Luther was taken away by his friends under the cover of darkness and hidden for nearly a year in a castle where the Roman Church could not get at him.

Most of the rest of Luther's story is part of Lutheran history, for as we will see in the next chapter, a second— quite different—branch of the Reformation would begin to grow in Switzerland. Because of the constant threat to his life if he ever left the little section of Germany where he had the protection of the local ruler, Frederick, Luther was not able to take the forefront and personally spread the truths at the heart of the Reformation himself.

A year later, he returned to Wittenberg and to his teaching post and pulpit, and sought to build the local church on the principles of the Reformation. It should not come as a surprise; he had many enemies even in the local congregation. During this period Luther suffered from periods of depression, and even—according to his own descriptions—great personal battles with Satan. Luther understood that Satan was not omniscient, and that he had many minions to do his bidding throughout the creation, while Satan himself could only work in one place at a time. No doubt in Luther's mind—that personal work was taking place in Wittenberg. So much so, that Luther would sit in his kitchen and have imaginary dialogues directly with the evil one.

His wife, Katie—a former nun—says that he was a hard man to live with (which is probably true of most preachers anyway!). She was a faithful, supportive wife who put up with a household full of students and admirers all the time. This is a picture not unlike the Swiss home of Francis Schaeffer at the end of the 20th Century, known as L'Abri.

By 1560, more than 20,000 students were trained at Wittenberg by Luther and his successor, Philip Melanchthon and thus the Lutheran branch of the Reformation took firm hold throughout Germany, and spread quickly to much of northern Europe—especially in the Scandinavian countries. Luther died at Eisleben on February 18, 1546, while on a trip to arbitrate a dispute between two Lutheran political leaders. He was buried in the Castle Church at Wittenberg.

In our next chapter, we will look at the growth of the very much separate, second branch of the Reformation, which involved a number of different men, and thus must properly be given a name other than that of a great hero!

## Chapter Four
## The Second Branch of the Reformation

I n Chapter Two we looked at some early attempts at Reformation. They came from various parts of the world: England, Czechoslovakia, Italy. In Chapter Three, we learned that the primary phase of real Reformation started in Germany under Luther. Parallel to Luther and just a little later in taking hold—and in many ways very different—was a second phase in Switzerland.

Most writers refer to this as the "Reformed branch" of the Reformation. Still today, one can track *all* protestant denominations to either the German (Lutheran) branch or the Swiss (Reformed) branch.

The Reformed branch does *not* begin with John Calvin, as many believe. Calvin came in the "second wave," a generation later. The Swiss branch began, instead, with a man named Ulrich Zwingli. Notice that the dates of his life, 1485-1531, are parallel with those of Luther.

Zwingli came to his Reformation views separate from Luther, which is why this truly is a separate branch of the Reformation. He was raised in the German speaking part of Switzerland in a wealthy family. He had a good humanist education (not to be confused with what is called today "atheistic humanism") and became a Roman Catholic priest. He was most greatly influenced by the leading Roman Catholic humanist named Erasmus, who stressed that scholars needed to read and understand the Greek New Testament—not for its theology, but as a great work of literature.

Zwingli also opposed the sale of indulgences in Zurich in 1518, but the results were much different from those in

Wittenberg. The town-folks simply laughed at his opposition. Perhaps he was not as dynamic and powerful a preacher as Luther. Who knows?

By 1519, Zwingli had become the pastor of a large church. He announced he would be preaching a series of sermons from the Bible. No biggie, right? Well, it was in those days. It was unheard of that a preacher would preach from the Bible! When the people heard the Word of God proclaimed, however, the results were fantastic. Again, the Reformation was, at its heart, a back-to-the-Bible movement.

Zwingli differed with Rome on a number of other issues as well. They included the rule about eating meat on Friday, the requirement of making pilgrimages, using what he referred to as idols in worship (which was the start of the later Iconoclast Movement). His basic view toward religious practice could be summed up in one sentence. If it is not authorized in Bible, it is forbidden for use in worship and religious practice. We will see later that this was the birth of the Regulative Principle of worship and the beginnings of Puritanism. Many people think the Puritans were offspring of Calvin. They did share his systematic theology, but what made them unique—the culture of the "puritanical"—sprang from Zwingli.

In 1523, there arose a big debate in Zurich over religious differences with Roman Catholics. The result was that Zwingli won over all the civil magistrates of the city and all the churches became Protestant. Zwingli tried to unite all the churches in other parts of Switzerland into one Reformation movement, but the Swiss city-states of those days were too independent. He also tried to unite with other aspects of the German Reformation, but he had too many differences with Luther. Luther disagreed on the Lord's Supper. The Anabaptists in Switzerland (whom we will soon discuss) disagreed on baptism and church government. The Swiss

Brethren, forefathers of today's Amish, believed in the complete separation of Church and State. So, unity was impossible.

This very lack of unity at the outset of the Reformation is the reason we have so many different denominations today. Had God been pleased to allow for unity during this period—and the leaders did indeed *try*, but failed—the course of world history would have been much different. I for one believe that it was not God's will for there to be unity among Protestant denominations. I do not know his reasons. I cannot say it was part of his prescriptive will (that is, he brought it to pass directly). But, I'm convinced this is the way God wanted it to be.

Ultimately Zwingli's influence in the theology of the Reformation can been seen beyond his early Puritan influence. He was the first to teach the need for biblical discipline in the true Church. Other Reformers, like Luther, saw the marks of a true Church as two—the faithful preaching of the Word and the proper administration of the Sacraments. Zwingli added biblical discipline as the third mark.

He also taught the importance of predestination in understanding the order of salvation. While others wanted to start with the work of Christ, Zwingli and his followers taught that we must start by understanding the decrees of God. This battle remains today between the two primary schools of Apologetics. The school known as Pre-Suppositionalists follow the teaching of Cornelius Van Til and others (Zwingli's view), and the school known as Historic follow the teaching of John Gerstner and R. C. Sproul.

Additionally, Zwingli stressed the need for understanding the work of the Holy Spirit in the inspiration of Scripture and in the distinction between the visible and invisible church.

A second important movement started parallel with the one begun by Zwingli. This did not follow a single person, but a group of varying views that historians refer to as the Radical Reformation. In different ways, they went *beyond* the Reformation, thus the title "Radical." The origins of this movement were also in Switzerland.

After a major debate with Zwingli in 1523, there remained a significant number of pastors of the newly Protestant churches who disputed the practice of infant baptism, which had continued in the Church since its New Testament inception. These men decided to proceed with adult baptism by re-baptizing each other. Then they began going about preaching believer baptism. Finally, one group began to practice immersion. This group became known as Anabaptists (which literally means "again Baptizers"). A large group of today's Baptists also comes from English Puritan roots, as we will see in a later chapter.

The practice of adult baptism began to stir up civil unrest in the cities of Switzerland and the local government officials ordered them charged with treason. For a few, a death sentence was pronounced which was carried out by drowning. (Talk about harsh and ironic!) Very quickly all others holding to this view moved to the area known as Moravia in southern Germany.

The growth of the Anabaptist movement was primarily among working class people. They followed the Reformed branch of theology more than the Lutheran branch—but were always more strict and severe in their religious practices. It is important to point out that, at this time, Anabaptists split from every branch and sub-branch of the Reformation.

We move on now to the third movement of the Reformed branch, that begun by John Calvin. He was born in 1509 and died in 1564, which you will note is a full generation after Luther. When Calvin appeared on the scene, the Reformation was fully in progress. That is why it is not proper to refer to this Reformed branch of the Reformation as Calvinism.

Calvin was raised in France. His father was a laborer who grew to white-collar status as a clerk and as an administrative secretary in a large Roman Catholic Church (notice the similarity to Luther in their economic backgrounds). As early as grade school, it was clear that Calvin had a brilliant mind.

At first, Calvin's father wanted him to study theology and become a priest, but later changed his mind and encouraged him to study law so he could make more money. Calvin entered college at age fourteen and immediately mastered the use of Latin. In those days, college life was much like Marine Corps boot camp is today, and Calvin thrived within that framework of discipline.

Although he was pretty much a typical Catholic boy when he entered college—which is to say somewhat religious in his life practices—he grew to become quite worldly. He discarded the Church and moved whole-heartedly into the secular, humanistic-philosophical answers that he found in his studies (much like Christians going to a liberal college today).

He entered law school rather than seminary at age eighteen, but he continued to study Greek part-time. He never explains in his writings why he did that, but one could easily surmise that his love for humanism, which brought with it a desire for learning in general, guided that at first.

After law school and the death of his father, Calvin returned to Paris in 1531 and studied to become a priest. In addition to his theological work, he studied more philosophy and took up Hebrew. During his time in Paris, he came under the influence of the university rector (like a campus minister today) named

Nicolas Cop. By 1533, Cop declared himself to be a disciple of Luther and had to flee Paris. His young disciples—including Calvin—also left Paris. Calvin continued to study and to write, demonstrating even in his early writings his convictions in Reformation issues.

For two or three years, Calvin moved around Western Europe, staying away from France for the most part, and changing his name from time to time. It was during this period that he wrote his first (of four) versions of his seminal work, *The Institutes of Christian Religion.* This was a short version, which he wrote anonymously.

Also during this period (most likely in 1533), he experienced something in his life which may well have been a conversion, although he makes only two simple references to it in his commentary on the Psalms—nothing like Luther's tower experience. He had been studying with some early Reformers in Strasburg, had returned to France, and in 1536 was heading back to Strasbourg or Basel when some battles in an ongoing regional war forced him to stop in Geneva for the night. By this time, Calvin had received some notoriety among the Reformers in Switzerland and one of the three pastors of the Protestant congregation in Geneva heard that Calvin was in town. The pastor's name was William Farel.

Farel tracked Calvin down at his lodging and had a meeting with him, which resulted in monumental changes not only in Geneva but also in Reformed circles for centuries to come. It reads best in Calvin's own words taken from the preface of his Commentary on the Psalms.

Because in order to go to Strasbourg, whither I now wished to retire, the most direct road was closed by the wars; I had planned to come this way quietly without stopping more than one night in the town. Only a little while before, the Papacy had been expelled from it by the means of this good person I have named [Farel] and of Master Pierre Viret: but things had not as yet been settled as to their form, and there were bad and dangerous divisions between those of the town.

Thereupon a certain person, who has now basely revolted and turned back to the Papists [du Tillet], discovered me and made me known to the others. Upon this Farel (burning as he was with a marvelous zeal to promote the gospel) instantly put forth all his efforts to detain me. And after having heard that I had several particular studies for which I wished to keep myself free, when he saw that he was gaining nothing by entreaties, he went so far as an imprecation, that it might please God to curse the reset and quietness I was seeking, if in so great a necessity I withdrew and refused aid and succor. Which word so horrified and shook me that I desisted from the journey I had undertaken: in such a way, however, that, feeling my shame and timidity, I did not want to commit myself to discharge any particular duty.

Although Farel and his friends had made great headway in teaching the principles of the Reformation and in starting three separate congregations in Geneva, Calvin stayed and became the real organizer and teacher for the city's churches. In Switzerland, the city government continued to control the churches, and ultimately Calvin came into conflict with the city council.

The biggest issues surrounded the administration of the Sacraments. The city council wanted everyone in the town to have access to the Sacraments—just as they had when the churches were Roman Catholic. But Calvin and his fellow ministers insisted that only those who had made a credible profession of faith in Jesus and who were not guilty of public, unrepentant sin could participate. Calvin refused to modify his stand and the council banished him from the city.

His first stay in Geneva had been only two years. He spent the next three years in Strasburg, serving as the pastor of the French-speaking congregation and working with a number of great Reformers—many from England and Scotland. During his three years in Strasburg, hard times fell upon the city of Geneva. Without the strong witness of the gospel, the people were living in open sin and lawlessness. With their hats in their hands, the city council came to Calvin and asked him to return.

He was given much more of a free hand this time to set up his own brand of church government—which he had learned as he and Martin Bucer had studied together at Strasbourg. Both became convinced of government by a plurality of elders. This was the first time in history that the form of government we recognize today as Presbyterianism was practiced.

Calvin went further than John Knox, the founder of Presbyterianism, did on the number of officers in the church. He said he saw four—pastors and teachers were separate offices (taking the language in Ephesians 4:11 to indicate two different offices rather than one, hyphenated office of pastor-teacher). To those two, he added elder and deacon. He viewed the three other offices listed in Ephesians 4:11 (apostle, prophet, and evangelist) as temporary offices only for the period of the New Testament. This issue is dealt with much more fully in my book, *Biblical Church Government.*

At first, Calvin still had some struggles with the council, again on the issue of the Sacrament of the Lord's Supper. In just the opposite way of three years earlier, the city council only wanted Sacraments administered once every month and Calvin wanted them administered in each congregation each week. Calvin compromised this time by having them administered in a different congregation each week so those who wanted to receive them weekly could do so.

Finally, the power shifted in the council and it came under control of Calvin's supporters. The last eight years of his life in Geneva, he was given a free hand to teach what he wanted. He then set up what he called an academy (what we would call a seminary) and many young men came to him to be trained for the pastorate. In a real sense, Calvin was *the* systematic theologian of the Reformation.

Throughout his life, he had many health problems— including hemorrhages, ulcers, arthritis, asthma and tuberculosis. He was known to be hot-tempered and even his appearance gave the impression of his being stern and forbidding. Those who knew him well, however, said he was warm-hearted and well loved.

Calvin's influence in Geneva was strong, but his influence, like Luther's, went far beyond the boundaries of that city. He lectured 200 times a year in his academy and through that means, thousands of students were influenced. Many English Reformers came to Geneva, and during one period of banishment from Scotland, Knox returned and began preaching to the English-speaking residents in the building next door to Calvin.

Calvin preached wrote commentaries on almost every book of the Bible. The *Institutes* were re-written three more times and were widely distributed throughout Europe and America. He wrote many more tracts and treatises. In fact, it takes up to sixty volumes to print all of his writing.

In a real sense, the influence of Calvin's writing continues until today. I, like many seminarians in Presbyterian-based schools, took a three-hour course where all we did was study the *Institutes*. When I was in the pastorate and writing weekly sermons, I usually had Calvin's Commentary on my desk along with some modern ones—and I would normally use it when the sermon was already finished just to make sure I hadn't messed up some idea of theology.

Geneva today celebrates its Reformed heritage with a great monument, the Wall of the Reformers. Conceived on a grand scale—it measures 325 feet long by 30 feet high. It was erected between 1909 and 1917. There are four enormous granite statues, which pay homage to the 16th Century religious movement, spearheaded by Guillaume (William) Farel, John Calvin, Théodore de Bèze and John Knox. The solemn fifteen-foot tall likenesses of the four reformers are flanked by smaller statues of major Protestant figures and inscriptions connected with the Reformation. Oliver Cromwell is surrounded by bas-reliefs of the Pilgrim fathers praying on the deck of the *Mayflower*. The 1689 presentation of the Bill of Rights to King William III by the English Houses of Parliament is also shown. Geneva's city motto *Post Tenebras Lux* (After darkness, light.), spreads over the whole structure.

In the next chapter, we will go back and look at the parallel time frame of the Reformation in Germany and at the effects in Switzerland as events unfolded in England. In the following chapter, we will see the parallel history in Scotland as we begin to focus directly on the historical roots of the PCA.

## Chapter Five
## The King Has No Son – The Beginnings of the Reformation in England

So far we have looked at the background of the Protestant Reformation in Europe—especially in Germany and Switzerland. We turn now to examine in more detail how this same spirit of Reformation was working out in the British Isles, since it is primarily there that we in the PCA find our heritage. Since we can't understand the Reformation in Scotland without looking first at what was happening in England, it is there we will begin.

It is hard for us to understand in our day and age, but we must see that both in Scotland and especially in England, the Reformation cannot be separated from political movements. In fact, it would be quite proper to say that the English Reformation was one of politics and not of theology. Nowhere is this any clearer than in the life of Henry the Eighth—who reigned through most of the first half of the 16th Century (1509-1547).

Henry was a good Catholic. In fact, he was given the title "Defender of the Faith" by one of the Popes for his strong attacks against Martin Luther. Pay attention when the next monarch is crowned in England in a few years—they still use that title for their King or Queen.

Henry is best known, of course, for his marriages. This is true far beyond the many portrayals we have seen in recent years in movies and on TV. Henry's basic problem started with his first wife—a lady (who had been married to Henry's older brother) named Catherine of Aragon. She did not bear Henry a son. The King honestly felt this was a sign of the lack of God's blessing upon the monarchy. (Still today we speak of the primary role of the King's wife being to bear him an "heir and a spare." Princess Diana did well in that role.)

There had been no sovereign, ruling queen in England for four centuries, so a son was essential. In 1526—about five years into his reign—Henry began to seek an annulment (divorce was not allowed in the Roman Catholic Church; it still is not allowed today). Henry sent the Archbishop of York, one of the most the senior Church officials in England, a Cardinal by the name of Wolsey, to Rome to try to arrange for the annulment, but he failed.

Henry would not give up, and made a very astute political decision. Cardinal Wolsey had not only been the Archbishop of Canterbury, he was also the Lord Chancellor (or Prime Minster) in the government. So during this same time frame (the actual years these events took place are a bit muddy, but this all occurs in the early 1530s), Henry fired Wolsey and appointed the first non-clergyman to the post of Lord Chancellor in history, Sir Thomas More. Sir Thomas was Speaker of the House of Commons.

Henry then called for the leading churchmen to discuss the theology of divorce and annulment. After a period of discussions, a priest named Thomas Cranmer, who had traveled extensively in Europe and had come under the influence of Luther and his followers (as well as marrying a young woman in Germany), turned out to be the most articulate spokesman for the position that Henry could indeed have a divorce. Henry quickly appointed Cranmer as his new Archbishop of Canterbury. In 1533, the English clergy declared Henry's marriage to Catherine of Aragon (we must use the full title, since three of Henry's six wives had the first name Catherine) to be terminated. Catherine of Aragon had borne

Henry one child that lived to become an adult—a girl named Mary whom we shall see again soon.

Thomas Cranmer then performed the wedding of Henry and his second wife, Anne Boleyn. (I'll leave the story of their romance that had been going on for some time to the tabloids!) His Lord Chancellor, Thomas More, would not support that decision and he was jailed. Thomas Cromwell took over his job. Anne Boleyn, by the way, did not bear Henry a son, but rather a daughter named Elizabeth. She, however, was not divorced—she was beheaded for adultery. It was Henry's third wife, Jane Seymour, who brought him the long-desired son, a boy named Edward.

In 1534, Henry had his Parliament pass what is known as the Act of Supremacy, which made the King the head of the Church of England instead of the Pope. This was the political act that brought Reformation to England—although you wouldn't know it if you went to church because nothing changed. The Church of England still held to almost all of the doctrinal positions as did Rome. When Sir Thomas More—remember he is in jail now—would not sign the Act of Supremacy, he was beheaded (as the movie *Man For All Seasons* so dramatically portrays).

Several good things were changed, however, including the abolishing of monasteries and turning Church-owned property over to the landowners. Also, there was a brilliant decision to allow the people to legally read the Bible in English (remember Wycliffe and his friends had previously been martyred for their efforts in this regard). While the movie didn't show this, Sir Thomas More was strongly opposed to this decision as well.

While nothing happened in the public realm on this issue, Henry did see the failure of the Catholic Church in the area of education of children and turned the education of his two children by Anne and Jane over to the Protestants. When we later see Edward and Elizabeth come to power, we will see the effects of this education bearing fruit.

Henry was, above all, a practical politician, who looked for a principle *after* he reached his goal. In the case of the Act of Supremacy, he found more in the principle than he had bargained for. He did not want Reformation, but in throwing off the authority of Rome, it came anyway.

Thomas Cranmer was in many ways the theological leader of the Reformation in England, although he never had the leadership skills of Luther or Calvin. In fact, one of the reasons that the Reformation was never fully effective in England is that there was not one great hero to lead the way. Cranmer was a college professor and a theologian first and foremost. He was elevated to Archbishop when he really didn't seek the post. Mostly, he was loyal to his King as a citizen, not as a theologian. He had already studied the teachings of Luther and the Reformers on the continent. He was more or less persuaded of the correctness of their stand. So much so, that Cambridge, where Cranmer taught, was called Little Germany by their detractors.

It wasn't until the death of Henry the VIII in 1547, when his nine-year-old son Edward VI came to the throne, that Cranmer could bring about the changes he desired in the Church. Cranmer was appointed the boy-king's principle advisor. He oversaw the writing of a new Prayer Book for the Church, which emphasized a broad-based worship service rather than one centering on the Eucharist.

Justification by Faith became a main tenant of the Church's theology. He continued to help get English translations of the Bible into the hands of the people. The Sacraments were reduced in number to the two Calvinistic forms. He oversaw the drafting of the 42 Articles of Faith (later to be reduced to 39) of the Church of England.

There had been a plan for Edward VI to wed Mary, Queen of Scots—thus uniting the two nations as well as the Protestant Reformation in both countries. However, seven years after coming to the throne, Edward, always a sickly child, died at age sixteen. This death had not only political but also religious significance—because his older half-sister Mary, who had been educated by a group of Spanish priests as a child (her mother had been a Spanish princess)—now came to the throne of England. And the teachings of the Roman Catholic Church came back with her—in spades.

Mary was very personable and she really was "the people's Queen." Actually, they probably pitied her because she had seemed to receive unfair treatment from her father and the political leaders during Edward VI's reign. There was a great political upheaval—fueled by the people—that brought her to the throne to replace Edward—the first queen to rule as sovereign since Matilda in the 12th Century.

Immediately upon her coronation, all Protestants who would not recant their teachings were arrested, jailed, and many burned at the stake or beheaded. Cranmer—the Archbishop—finally stood up to a politician and for his trouble was arrested and thrown in a cell with many other famous martyrs. While he was in jail, many of these men were burned at the stake, some even in view of Cranmer's cell. Every historian has an account of these events. The following is taken from James Atkinson's work, *The Great Light* (Grand Rapids: 1968, Eerdmans):

Cardinal Pole then ordered the prisoners to be tried for heresy. John Rogers, the translator of the Bible, was the first to go to the stake. The common English people did not like this; Rogers was cheered to his death. The envoy of Charles V warned Pole of the dangerous folly of this procedure. Persecutors always overreach themselves. Hooper, Saunders, Taylor, Ferrar and others lengthened the line of this noble army of martyrs. Ridley, the scholar, and Latimer, the preacher (now an old man) were proceeded against and burnt on October 16, 1555, in Broad Street Oxford, a painful scene witnessed by Cranmer from the tower of his prison. Ridley, who in good conscience had spent the previous night in quiet rest and peace with God suffered unspeakable agonies owing to the dampness of the wood. It was at that moment that the elderly Latimer, a preacher even in his death, uttered words, which belong to every schoolboy's repertoire: "Be of good comfort, Master Ridley, and play the man. We shall this day light such a candle, by God's grace, in England, as I trust shall never be put out."

Cranmer, having witnessed these deaths, and being a humble, weak, and old man—felt there was little to be served to the cause of Christ and so he agreed with some of Mary's followers to recant some of his Protestant positions. We must not be too quick to judge this action, as all along Cranmer had held a loyalty to the throne that almost resembled his loyalty to the Word of God. He had a real struggle in dividing his loyalties.

But even though he had signed a statement of recanting, he was still ordered burned at the stake. This also is from Atkinson's work:

So far all proceedings were running according to plan. He was now expected to conclude with a declaration of the Queen's just title to the crown and a retraction of his books and writings on the sacraments. But he continued, speaking of his previous recantings:

…which writings now here I renounce and refuse, as things written with my own hand, contrary to the truth which I thought in my heart, and written for fear of death, and to save my life, if it might be. And that is, all such bills and papers which I have written or signed with my hand since my degradation; herein I have written many things untrue. And forasmuch as my hand offered, writing contrary to my heart, my hand shall first be punished therefore; for, may I come to the fire, it shall be first burned.

And as for the Pope, I refuse him, as Christ's enemy and Antichrist, with all his false doctrine. And as for the sacrament, I believe as I have taught in my book against the Bishop of Winchester; the which my book teaches so true a doctrine of the sacrament, that it shall stand at the last day before the judgment of God, where the papistical doctrine, contrary thereto, shall be ashamed to show her face.

An uproar broke out. Cranmer was pulled down from the stage. He virtually ran to the fire with the Spanish friars shrieking at him to make one last recantation. These he ignored. At the scaffold he stood in his shirt barefooted and bareheaded on that cold, wet March, day, as steadfast as the stake to which he was chained. He shook hands with a few bystanders. When the wood was kindled and began to burn fire, and in that heroic deed gave voice to his undying faith. With the words of Stephen "Lord Jesus, receive my spirit" he went forth from this life with the dignity of the ancient martyrs.

This only goes to show that you don't have to be a hero to be a martyr.

In all, about 300 people were burned at the stake by Mary Tudor, or Bloody Mary as the Queen is known in history. Many more suffered horribly and died in prison because of their allegiance to Jesus. It was only through the grace of God that England was kept from further disaster under the reign of Bloody Mary. She was taken sick and died after reigning only five years.

Her half sister, Elizabeth the First, came to the throne. You may recall she had been raised by Protestants and had been under guard in England during Mary's reign. Elizabeth was nowhere as pretty as her older sister (and some felt not as smart). Although she is now remembered as a great Queen, she was very shy and during her reign did not pursue the outward perks of the monarchy but rather served more behind the scenes, often as a shrewd politician.

Clearly, God's providence that put her on the throne at that time. Her decisions were always those of compromise. She accepted some of the Protestant Reformation, but did not disallow all belief in Catholic doctrines. However, she did remove allegiance from Rome and she herself took over as governor of the Church, thus requiring that all new bishops be installed. Since the ones in power at that time had been installed by Rome, this brought significant change to the leadership of the Church. To her credit, she accomplished all of this without the same level of killing. About 300 Roman Catholics were killed over her forty-five year reign, but these deaths were primarily for political reasons (treason) rather than religious issues.

Without going into much detail here, we can see how the Anglican Church of today began as a compromise between Rome and Reformation, and never reached the same level of change as did the churches in Europe and in Scotland.

## Chapter Six
## The Birth of Presbyterianism – The Reformation In Scotland

**P**arallel with what we have been studying in England, Switzerland and Germany, the Reformation was making the slightest of beginnings in Scotland. At the outset, we must understand that Scotland before the Reformation was in worse shape than any European country. It undoubtedly suffered with the worst morality of any nation's clergy. The Archbishop of St. Andrews had twenty *registered* children (remember, priests were forbidden to marry), and these were just the ones he admitted to!

Scotland had terrible economic conditions as well. By this time. the Catholic Church owned over half the land in Scotland, and the most of the rest was owned by the Stuart kings and their relatives.

The social and political situation was chaos. While the Stuarts had ruled for some time, they had little power and the people were bickering whether to side with England or side with France to overthrow the Stuart kings so they could improve their economic position. I cannot imagine a worse place to live than Scotland at the beginning of the 16th Century.

Because of the horrible educational institutions, most of the brightest young people studied in Europe, which means that they came in contact with the teachings of Martin Luther and the Reformation. One of these young men was Patrick Hamilton (1503-1528).

Hamilton was of royal blood, related to James V, the reigning Stuart King, and to several other Dukes and the like. As a youth, he had received an Abbacy, which means he inherited the position of Abbot for a town in Scotland. He did not have to serve as a clergyman to receive the pay however; he could hire someone to carry out the duties for a salary far less than what he received. Remember, this was the standard in England and Scotland in those days.

Hamilton at first went to Paris to study, where his primary influences were Erasmus and Luther. (Please note he was in Paris at least ten years prior to Calvin.) He returned to Scotland while still a teenager, with some of his Lutheran views but quickly saw he would not get anywhere and returned to Europe, this time to study in Wittenberg and Marburg directly under Luther and his followers. In 1527, he was ready to return to Scotland.

He began to find public venues in which he could teach (well, I guess he was really preaching even though he wasn't a clergyman). He quickly gathered a following of people. Since he was the King's nephew, the Church wanted to proceed carefully, so the Archbishop of St. Andrews invited him to a conference. Being a youth without fear, Hamilton attended. As a result of this conference, and several others in which he clearly revealed his Protestant views, he was arrested and taken to jail.

After a quick trial while the King was out of the country, in which Hamilton refused to recant anything, he was declared to be a heretic and scheduled for execution. They carried out the sentence the same day as the trial, again fearful that the King might intervene. They took him out to the stake in front of old St. Andrews College.

As Hamilton was led to the stake, he reportedly said something like this to a servant, "...I have no more to leave thee but the example of my death which, I pray thee, keep in mind; for albeit the same be bitter and painful in man's judgment, yet it is the entrance to everlasting life, which none can inherit who deny Christ before this wicked generation."

The first time they tried to light the fire it didn't take and Hamilton received only minor burns. So, he just kept on preaching, calling people to repent of their sins. The second attempt to light the fire succeeded, and standing in the fast growing flames Hamilton cried out, "How long shall darkness overwhelm this realm? How long wilt thou suffer this tyranny of men? Lord Jesus, receive my spirit."

Over the next several decades, about twenty more preachers came along, gathered a following, and were quickly arrested by the church officials, brought to a quick trial, and most of them were burned at the stake. The most successful of these was named George Wishart.

George Wishart was another son of a wealthy family, related to many of the great landowners who supported the King. He left Scotland to attend college in France and returned to Scotland in 1532 where he taught Greek at a school in Montrose (a town between Aberdeen and Dundee on the east coast). But like Hamilton before him, the religious ideas he had picked up in Europe aroused suspicion among church leaders, so he moved to England. It wasn't long before he was in trouble again. He began preaching against the Roman Catholic Church there and had to move back to Europe.

He went to Germany and a bit later on to Switzerland, where he translated the First Helvetic Confession into English. In 1543, he returned to England as a teacher at Cambridge (which you will recall had become known as Little Germany).

About this time, there was a delegation from England to Scotland to try to arrange a marriage for the young Prince Edward, who would shortly become king, with Mary, Queen of Scots. Wishart wisely chose to travel back to Scotland with this group to avoid any immediate troubles. He moved to Dundee—across the bay from St. Andrews—and started openly preaching against Roman Catholicism.

Well, Church authorities followed their normal path and moved to action quickly. They used their political pressure to require the city council to expel him from Dundee. This forced him to move to the less densely populated area of southwest Scotland, below Glasgow, where he still gathered a large following—this time not just of poor folks, but of some of his relatives in the nobility.

While in the southwest, word came back that an episode of the plague had broken out in Dundee, so he went back to try to help comfort the dying. At the end of that summer, he returned again to the southwest and began preaching. While there, he met a young man who was a tutor in the household of some close friends—a young fellow by the name of John Knox, who served as his bodyguard, carrying a two-handed sword.

Finally, the church leaders realized they had to act and the Archbishop of St. Andrews persuaded several of the nobility that Wishart should be arrested. Just after he had convinced Knox to return to his job as a tutor (and in God's providence, in the knick of time) Wishart was arrested. Back at St. Andrews, he was tried, convicted of heresy, and before they took him out to be burned—he was strangled in order to keep him from preaching while he was being put to death.

For some reason, Wishart's martyrdom had more of an impact on Scotland than the twenty or more that preceded him. It was a major factor to stir up John Knox to step up to take leadership of the Protestant movements. And it also aroused many Protestants and even Protestant sympathizers who were still on the fence, theologically speaking, to hate the Church leaders—most especially Cardinal Beaton—and ultimately it was this movement that brought about the murder of Beaton himself.

John Knox is known as the father of Presbyterianism and the title is properly suited when one sees the almost miraculous way God protected him throughout his ministry in Scotland. Like so many of the heroes of the Reformation, Knox was born into a middle class family involved in farming (essentially the only industry in the country) about 1505 in a small town near Edinburgh. He most likely attended university at nearby St. Andrews College where he studied for the ministry and was ordained as a priest in 1536.

For reasons not really clear in the historical record, he did not receive an assignment as a parish priest. Perhaps the leaders of the Roman Catholic Church had already recognized he had been influenced by the Lutheran doctrine that most certainly had arrive at St. Andrews by the time Knox completed his studies in 1536. Or, just as likely, his family was probably too poor to purchase a position for him, as was common at the time. At any rate, we find him doing whatever he can to make ends meet—including becoming a tutor for some lower-level Scottish nobility. It was while he was serving in one of those families in the southwestern area of Scotland that he came under the influence of some early Reformers and ultimately of George Wishart's preaching. As we have already seen, he became one of Wishart's bodyguards.

In 1546 when Cardinal Beaton, the Archbishop of St. Andrews and the leader of the Roman Catholic Church in Scotland, made the decision to silence George Wishart through the barbaric acts of strangling and burning him at the stake, his followers could take no more. A small band of men (less than twenty by most accounts) stormed the castle at St. Andrews where Beaton lived, assassinated him and mutilated his body.

Since Scotland was closely aligned with France—both through the Church and through political intrigue (remember Henry the VIII had broken off relationships with Rome by this time)—the castle was brought under siege by a group of French ships trying to wrestle control away from the rebel Protestants. Although Knox had earlier escaped capture by just a few hours, he now felt he should join the rebels and was able to join them in the castle.

In an episode that rivals Farel's call of Calvin to stay in Geneva, one of the preachers in the castle—during a Protestant worship service—publicly challenged Knox to assume the role of pastor of the congregation of rebels. With some trepidation, he agreed and thus stepped into the shoes of a preacher of the Reformation.

His ministry there was quickly ended within a few months when the French forces reclaimed the castle and took all the rebels captive. Some were thrown in jail in Scotland; others, including Knox, were used as galley slaves (on rowing ships) in the French fleet. Knox spent nearly two years in this capacity before a political deal was worked out between England and France that allowed Knox to be exiled to England. Edward VI was now on the throne and the Protestants had sufficient power in England to bring this about.

Knox immediately assumed the role of a pastor in an English congregation just south of the border with Scotland and most of his worshippers on Sunday were Scots who crossed the border to hear him preach. This caused him to be viewed as a troublemaker by the Church of England and he was moved to a congregation in London where they could keep a closer eye on him.

This failed to truly silence Knox (as others would fail in the future). He preached boldly in favor of the authority of Scripture and the continued errors in practice in the Church of England. Some political leaders liked what they heard and invited him to become Chaplain to the throne and have the opportunity to preach before the young King. But most of the church leaders were not as enamored with his activities and did all they could to silence him—which was very difficult because of his personal popularity. At one point they offered him the opportunity to be a bishop, which would take him away from regular preaching and effectively silence him, but he refused since he did not recognize bishops as a lawful office (a position that would become important a bit later).

About this time young King Edward died and his older sister, Mary Tudor (Bloody Mary) assumed the throne. This meant that all committed Protestants instantly became *personae non grates* and Knox (with many others) fled to the continent. We should not think that Knox fled for fear of dying. Rather, England was not his heart's concern and he wanted to remain alive to ultimately return to Scotland.

In Europe, he initially went to Frankfurt. He later moved to Geneva when Calvin returned there and became the pastor of the English-speaking congregation. Calvin writes of Knox as a "brother…laboring energetically for the faith." Knox returned the kindness speaking of Geneva and especially of Calvin's work in the city as "the most perfect school of Christ that was ever on earth since the days of the apostles."

As his desire was always to return to Scotland, Knox made one attempt at return in 1555, but it lasted only six months because of constant danger of captivity. His friends insisted that he return to Geneva. Knox ultimately moved to a town on the coast of France and planned for his return to Scotland from there. Obviously many of the Protestant supporters from Scotland would come there to meet with him in the development of these plans.

During this period on the continent, Knox became a prolific writer. The most famous of his writings was a book entitled *The First Blast of the Trumpet against the Monstrous Regiment of Women*. The subject matter and the sexist nature of the very title have resulted in Knox being greatly defiled in history. In fact, while I lived in Scotland in the early 1960s (long before becoming a Christian, let alone a Presbyterian), I learned that it is common practice to walk on the sidewalk along the graveyard at St. Giles (where his remains are buried) and spit on the gravestone. We must remember that in the heat of the day, with Mary Tudor lighting the skies of England with the burning bodies of Reformers, and with another woman, Mary of Lorraine, on the throne of Scotland during the French occupation, who was also persecuting Protestants, he had some justification. Later in life, Knox admitted his book was rude and ill timed.

As with all such mistakes in judgment that people make, "what goes around, comes around." When Mary Tudor finally died and her half-sister, the Protestant-educated Elizabeth, came to the throne, she never trusted Knox in Scotland because she thought the book was also aimed at her, which it was not.

Knox was most definitely not a woman hater. In fact, if he had a problem in his life, it was that he had too many close friends among women. Most of his financial supporters were wealthy women. Not that there is any evidence of sexual immorality, but when he finally married late in life, he married a girl who was the daughter of his best friend—a woman—in order to continue his close friendship and counsel with this woman.

Finally, in 1559, at the age of fifty-four, Knox returned to Scotland. The battle was still raging. Although political history is fascinating, we only have time for a quick summary. Mary of Lorraine (sometimes referred to as Mary of Guise) was a French princess who married James V, King of Scotland. They had a daughter, Mary Stewart (or Mary Stuart to use the French form of the name) who at the age of six assumed the right of the throne of Scotland when James V died. Her mother wanted her to return to France, however, and marry into that royal family. So she sent Mary to France where, at age sixteen, she did exactly that. In the meantime, Mary of Lorraine remained in Scotland as the Regent.

When Knox returned to Scotland, Mary of Lorraine was still ruling and completely committed to her alliances with France. The Protestants had gathered an army to seek to overthrow her, and this army took on the name of The Congregation. It was sort of like a mobile church, with officers and a constitution based on the Bible alone. In a real sense, the hierarchy of Presbyterianism was worked out on the battle field!

The army traveled around the countryside and destroyed many church buildings because they still had altars, icons and other vestments of the Church of Rome. Needless to say, they were hotly pursued all the time by the Queen's army. Knox immediately became, at the same time, the leader of the army and the pastor of The Congregation upon his return.

In 1560, Mary of Lorraine died. Her son-in-law (rather than her daughter, Mary Stuart) had previously risen to the throne of France, but he had died. Political intrigue in France brought

Mary Stuart's brother-in-law (her husband's brother) to the throne, so her only alternative was to return to Scotland to assume the position of queen she had held *in absentia* for so many years. She is from then on in history known as Mary, Queen of Scots.

By this time, Elizabeth had come to the throne in England and sensed that it was of political importance that the French *not* take control of Scotland, so she sent troops to help the rebels in Scotland. With these troops on their side, The Congregation fought a great battle on the England-Scotland border, near the town of Leith. While there was no decisive victory, the support from England revitalized The Congregation.

By July of 1560, it was clear that the French could not prevail and a peace treaty was signed at Leith. All foreign troops (English and French) left Scotland and the Parliament was called and instructed to be open to the religious teachings of the Protestants. It was a great victory for The Congregation and for John Knox in particular. Mary, Queen of Scots left for France in disgrace.

The Scottish Church had great growth for a year, but then Mary was allowed to return to Scotland in 1561. As we saw in England, the same split allegiances of the people between church and their royalty occurred, and a political battle ensued for many years. This battle was fought principally between Queen Mary and John Knox.

Knox knew that Mary was a devout Roman Catholic herself and would always work to bring the Catholic Church back into Scotland. In fact, he was aware all this time that she had priests in the castle conducting private masses for her in secret. Many other leaders did not know that, however, and sought to work out a compromise. Scottish historian A. M.

Renwick gives this interesting glimpse into this situation in his now out-of-print book *The Story of the Scottish Reformation* (Grand Rapids: Eerdmans, 1950):

> One of the most dramatic episodes in the life of Knox was when the Queen had him summoned before the Council towards the end of 1563 and charged with treason. He was accused of 'convocatin the liges' because he had sent out a circular letter at the request of the Church asking them to attend in Edinburgh to secure justice for two Protestants who were on trial on a charge of riotous behavior. It was a most serious occasion. Knox had no one in the Council to support him. If they voted against him, his life would be in jeopardy. The Earl of Moray and Lethington tried to persuade him to confess his guilt and cast himself on the queen's mercy. He absolutely refused. Lethington then tried to catch him with subterfuges but found the Reformer could not be so easily deceived. The trial then proceeded.
>
> Mary felt that at last she had Knox in her power. In her elation she forgot her queenly dignity. "When she saw John Knox standing at the other end of the table, bareheaded, she first smiled and after gave a gaulf of laughter, whereat placeboes ('yes-men') 'gave their plaudit.' Then, speaking in excellent Scots, she said 'But wot ye whereat I laugh? Yon man made me greet (weep) and grat never a tear himself. I will see if I can gar (compel) him greet.'"
>
> Knox acknowledged he had written the letter and declined a request from the Council to withdraw it. In reply to the chargers read out by Lethington, he gave an able disquisition on lawful and unlawful assemblies,

which impressed the Council. When he proceeded to show the danger of allowing the Roman Church to gain the ascendancy again, he was interrupted—probably by Lethington—with the words: "You forget you are not now in the pulpit." Promptly came the historic reply, "I am in the place where I am demanded by conscience to speak the truth, and therefore the truth I speak, impugn it whoso list."

To keep a long story short, there was much controversy until Queen Mary was involved (as most people think) in a plot to murder her husband so she could marry someone else (*à la* Henry the VIII himself)! As a result of this plot and killing, and not because of any religious issues, Mary was jailed and in 1567 abdicated the throne to her infant son who became King James VI. This was a great victory for Knox and the Presbyterians.

The next year Mary escaped from prison and fled to England. There for nineteen years, she plotted to overthrow not only the ruler (her own son, mind you) in Scotland, but also Elizabeth in England. Finally, Elizabeth had her put to death for treason in 1587.

John Knox was able to lead the formation of the Church of Scotland into the very first Presbyterian denomination. He drafted a Book of Discipline for the Scottish Church in which Calvin's system of church government in Geneva was adopted. Each local church was to have a pastor along with a group of elders (we now call this group a Session), elected by the congregation. Regional groups of churches known as presbyteries were also set up, with an even larger group of elders, which became known as Synods. The annual meeting of the entire Church was known as the General Assembly. All of these terms are still in use today.

Knox also greatly influenced change in the style of worship for the Church as well. A lot of what he brought into Scotland he had worked out in Geneva along with Calvin much earlier in his life. He adopted Zwingli's principle (known today as the Regulative Principle) that if a practice could not be found in the Bible it must not be used in worship in the Church. He made sure the Church did not celebrate any of the holy days or feast days that were so prevalent in the Roman Catholic Church—only the Sabbath day. And, of course, expository preaching became the hallmark of the Scottish Church.

After Mary's departure, Knox settled in as the pastor of St. Giles Church in Edinburgh. He also wrote the first history of the Reformation in Scotland himself, which made a wonderful resource for all future historians to use. (It makes one think that those of us involved in the beginning of the Presbyterian Church in America should at least write our own memoirs.)

Sadly, within a few years after Mary left the throne and relative peace prevailed in the Church, Knox suffered a stroke (in 1570) which restricted his active participation in the work of the Church. He even moved out of Edinburgh to quieter surroundings in St. Andrews, but his influence remained strong. The following except from the diary of James Melville, a student at St. Andrews (*not* the author of Moby Dick), helps us understand how:

> Of all the benefits I had that year (1571) was the coming of that maist notable prophet and apostle of our nation, Mr. John Knox, to St. Andrews. I heard him teach there the prophecies of Daniel. I had my pen and my little book, and tuk away sic things as I could comprehend......Mr. Knox wald sumtyme come in and repose him in our college-yard and call us scholars to him and bless us, and exhort us to know God, and his

work in our country, and stand by the guid caus. I saw him everie day of his doctrine (preaching) go hulie and fear (slowly and warily) with a furring of martriks about his neck, a staff in the ane hand, and guid godlie Richart Ballenden, his servand, halding up the other oxtar (armpit) from the Abbey to the paroche kirk, and by the said Richart and another servnd, lifted up to the pulpit.

The next year (1572) Knox was well enough to return to his pulpit at St. Giles for a time, but by the end of the year his health faded again. Knowing the end of his ministry was coming, he led the church in a search for his successor. He preached his last sermon in early November at the installation of the new pastor. By the end of the month he had died.

Standing at his graveside after the funeral, The Earl of Morton—who was then serving then as the Regent or advisor to the young King James, and who was no great friend of the Protestants—said these most remarkable words that summarize the story of Knox's life: "Here lies one who neither flattered nor feared any flesh."

## Chapter Seven
## The Writing of Church Confessions – Dordt and Westminster

Our topic in this chapter is the writing of church confessions. Because of the length of this topic, we will focus primarily on the two that are the most important in the historical roots of the PCA—the Synod of Dordt and the Westminster Confession of Faith.

While there is not time to cover them, here is a list of some of the other most significant confessions written in the 16th Century:

- Lutheran Confession of Augsburg (1530, written by Melanchthon)
- Book of Common Prayer with 42 Articles (1549, written by Cranmer)
- French Reformed Confession (1559, first draft written by Farel, adopted by a larger group)
- Belgic Confession (1561, written by Guy du Bray)
- Heidelberg Catechism (1563, written by German ministers who had been influenced by Calvin, and therefore reflects Reformed teachings).

We must understand the role of a confession to begin with. The word "confess," used in this way, comes from the Latin *confiteri*, meaning to publicly praise. Therefore, a confession of faith is a public profession of one's convictions and thanks to God.

The similar term, "creed," comes from the Latin verb *credo,* which means primarily "I place confidence in" or "I rely upon." A better English translation for the original Latin of the beginning of the Apostle's Creed would be "I trust in God, the Father Almighty."

Creeds and confessions tend to be produced in times of trial—periods when the author or authors are under stress or attack, and thus it is important to spell out a position. That was the case with the creeds that were developed by the very early church councils—and also with the confessions of faith that were produced in the early years of the Protestant Reformation.

Most people say that in the 21$^{st}$ Century we do not live in a creed or confession-writing period of history. I tend to agree. That is why so many people are reluctant to make any changes to the Church standards of the Church, although clearly there are some areas in which we could make some improvement.

Along with confessions of faith, we need to mention the special place of catechisms. A catechism is a teaching device, dating back to the Greek philosophers, whereby a specific question is asked and answered, and the student needs to learn the importance of the question as well as the answer. Catechisms were important throughout church history. Initially they were used in the Church as a way of training a new convert preparing to make a public profession of faith at the time of baptism. They were later used in "confirmation class" by those who had been baptized as infants. During the time of the Reformation, they were used as a good way to teach important theology—both to young people and to adults (even church officer candidates).

To understand the Synod of Dordt and its confessional statement, we must begin with some background on the Reformation in the Netherlands. You should understand that the Dutch and Scottish churches have always held much in common—even up to today.

The Reformed churches in the Netherlands always had the reputation for wide tolerance of different beliefs—even in the early days. But as political struggles grew—especially against Spain and the strength of that nation's Roman Catholic churches—the churches in the Netherlands became increasingly more reformed by the end of the 16th Century. However, they did not write their own doctrinal statements. Rather, they adopted those from neighboring countries—such as the Heidelberg Catechism (written in Germany but with a strong Swiss, Calvinistic influence) and a confession from Belgium (also strongly influenced by Swiss Calvinists).

During this period, a brilliant scholar named Jacob Hermans, who changed his name in adulthood to Jacob Arminius, was studying in Geneva under Theodore Beza, Calvin's successor. Beza, as is often the case with disciples who follow a prominent teacher, was more strict and more severe in his theological positions than was his teacher. Arminius was called to become a pastor in the Reformed churches in the Netherlands. To assume this position, he had to be examined and approved by the Church (which is standard practice yet today for ministers).

Arminius had trouble with the 16th Article of the Belgic Confession, which asserts that God is *both* merciful and just. He is merciful toward those whom he has elected in Jesus *and* he is just by leaving others in sin and perdition. Many members of Presbyterian churches today struggle with that same issue. Arminius argued against this teaching and quite clearly approached the whole process of how salvation takes place from the point of view of how it appears to man. While Calvinism—upon which the Belgic Confession is based—looks at the process from the eyes of God, Arminius would argue from the perspective of how it would look to him, to mankind, rather than through God's eyes. Although he disagreed with this article, Arminius promised the Church upon his acceptance that he would not teach against the standards of the Church—even though he himself did not hold to those standards—and he was accepted on that basis. This is also a common practice in the church today—especially for issues that do not strike at the "vitals of religion."

However, in 1603, Arminius was elected to be a professor of theology at the University of Leiden and the trouble began. He broke his promise and began to teach his contrary views. As a result of his teaching, many young ministers became convinced of his position—resulting in a major division among the students and faculty. Just six years later, Arminius died, having himself never raised a formal question in the Church. However, the same could not be said of his followers.

This group of followers had strong backing from politicians, especially from a man aspiring to become Prime Minister, named Grotius. In 1610, they drew up their formal theological position, which they called the Remonstrance. These articles set forth the areas in which they disagreed with the position of the Belgic Confession. It is worth noting that they agreed with everything else. It is also important to note that this is the very first break from all the early confessions written during the 16th Century, which were all similarly based on the Swiss teaching begun by Calvin. There were five areas, five points if you will, of the disagreement.

First, the followers of Arminius, forever after known as Arminians (which should be pronounced so as not to confuse the word with "Armenian," referring to people living in the area of Armenia near Turkey—one is "r-min-ian," the other is "r-mean-ian"), believed that election (or predestination) was conditional upon an individual's belief and obedience in the future. They claimed that salvation is man's choice, and that God has foreknowledge of who will choose salvation, rather than it being unconditional (thereby based only on God's will).

Second, they believed that the Atonement (Jesus substitutionary death on the cross) was intended for, as well as sufficient for, all human beings and for every human being, but it may not apply to all if the grace of God was resisted.

Third, they believed that man had the ability to participate in the expression of saving faith, rather than being in a state of total depravity and totally unable to do any spiritual work in his own behalf.

Fourth, they believed that man has the ability to resist grace that was offered by God through the gospel and thereby make a choice through their own participation as to whether to believe in Jesus or not.

Finally, they believed that no one was able to have certain assurance of their salvation and therefore it was possible to fall from a position of saving grace.

While there had been many previous attempts to have a decision made on these issues, by 1617, there were just about an equal number of ministers in Holland who were Arminians as there were those who were Calvinists. The Remonstrants sought a Synod meeting of the leaders of the Church in Holland as well as nearby Lutherans (who would be friendly to them on several of their points).

The Prime Minister of the Netherlands, who himself leaned toward Arminianism, compromised by calling a national Synod, but invited representatives from Reformed churches in

England, France, Switzerland, and parts of Germany to give advice (but they could not vote). We must always remind ourselves that during this period of church history there was a very strong connection between the activities of the political state and the Church.

The Synod began in November of 1618 and went on for a full six months. This was probably the most respectable, most knowledgeable Reformed body every called with representation from throughout the Protestant world. The purpose of the Synod was *not* to be an open forum, however. The purpose was to defend the standing doctrinal views of the Church in the Netherlands against the attack of the Remonstrants.

It would be nice to report that there was a total gentlemanly discussion of the great theological issues and that the decision was arrived at without emotional passion. But that was not (and to this day continues not to be) the way the decision was reached. The Remonstrants tried in every possible way to upset the Synod through internal political maneuvers. Ultimately, the leader of this group became so intolerable in his attitudes, his standing as a member of the Synod was revoked and he was physically barred from attending further deliberations.

The final response of the Synod—which took place in the town of Dordt—was to adopt four canons that defended the attack of the Remonstrants. The result has come to be known throughout church history as the Five Points of Calvinism because the Remonstrants had raised five points. But even as we list these points, we must be reminded that these are not the full summary of Calvinism, but rather the points raised as an objection to a small part of this branch of theology.

74

The resulting Canons of Dordt reaffirmed what was taught in the Belgic Confession and all other Reformed confessions of the 16th Century. That can be summarized under these five points:

1. Total Depravity
2. Unconditional Election
3. Limited Atonement
4. Irresistible Grace
5. Perseverance of the Saints

Because the first letter of each point can be used to spell the very Dutch flower known as a T-U-L-I-P this has stuck over the centuries as the order and phraseology—although number 3 could be better named Particular Atonement.

As well as affirming these responses, the Synod also reaffirmed the full authority of the Belgic Confession and the Heidelberg Catechism. They also deposed more than 200 ministers from their denomination. All the acts of the Synod were confirmed by an actual vote of the civil government in the Netherlands. One of the Arminian leaders was later beheaded for treason against the government. The aspiring politician Grotius was imprisoned also for treason.

The Canons of Dordt were accepted as consistent with the Bible by *all* other Reformed bodies in the world—except England—where we return to understand the background of the Westminster Assembly and the resulting Confession of Faith and Catechisms. Turning now to Westminster, recall in Chapter Five we discussed the fact that Queen Elizabeth came to the throne after the bloody phase of the Reformation under Mary Tudor. This brought some freedom to the Protestants, but not real Reformation.

Elizabeth was not very strongly religious herself, and wanted more than anything to work out a peaceable compromise between Roman Catholics and Protestants. She continued many of the practices of her father, Henry VIII. She broke formal ties with Rome, but continued what she considered a "Catholic" Church in England with herself as the head. She kept some of the traditions and forms of worship from the Roman Catholics. The major problem was that she would not give control of the government of the Church to the leaders of the Church, but rather maintained political control with herself and her political advisors. It was in this context that a group who became known as the Puritans arose (we'll get to them momentarily).

Suffice it to be said at this point that a minister who would not conform to the standards of the Church of England under Elizabeth was subject to persecution. This was true even though at the time of her death in 1603, many of the people—at least the common people—believed in Puritan principles. When Elizabeth died her successor to the throne was King James VI of Scotland, who became known as King James I of England. He had been raised as a Presbyterian in Scotland and so the Puritans hoped that he would really bring in the Reformation when he assumed the throne in England.

However, as England's King, James followed the advice of the leaders of the established Church. He even increased pressure upon the non-conformist ministers (as they became commonly known) and with the controversy over Arminianism on the continent, allowed the entrance of this doctrine into the life of the English church. This forced some of the non-conformists to leave England. It is at this time that a group of Puritans, who later became known as Pilgrims, left England and moved to the Netherlands. This same group ultimately sailed to the shores of North America and established the Plymouth Colony, resulting in the founding of America—by

Calvinists who had been persecuted for their beliefs and practices.

Throughout his reign, James I refused to listen to the voice of the people who desired freedom of religion. Clearly the vast majority wanted it. When he died in 1625, he had dismissed four parliaments who had tried to bring about change for religious freedom.

His successor, Charles I—also reared in Presbyterian Scotland—also chose to listen to the bishops of the established Church, and initiated an even more severe period of persecution. Any minister who failed to conform to the regulations of the established Church, which now had all kinds of Catholic rituals—even certain prayer books, clothing (known as vestments) and drapings from the pulpits to which the minister must adhere—would be put out of the Church. It was during the reign of Charles I that the largest number of Christians left England for America and religious freedom. Clearly, America was founded by people seeking freedom from government control in the practice of their religion.

Now, just who were these Puritans? There isn't time to go into great detail, but I think a summary of some of the main positions will help us to understand them. Just as in the Reformation in Europe (but had never taken hold in England), the Puritans held to the primacy of Scripture. This means that the Scriptures are at the center of all things that exist—including the Church, the State, individual life, all spheres of community life. The Puritans believed to a degree in what has become known over the centuries as Sphere Sovereignty.

Secondly, the Puritans held to the twin marks of individual holiness and the sovereign grace of God. As consistent Calvinists, they began all their theology with God. (Recall that the Arminian approach to theology always begins with man.)

Puritans saw the necessity that if God is sovereign, then Christians must be holy. They held a very high view of sanctification in individual lives. This is very clear in the Westminster Larger Catechism as it spells out details of the Ten Commandments, Sabbath observance and things such as that.

The third principle of Puritanism is the utter sinfulness of man. This was an underlining of the First Point of Calvinism concerning total depravity. Theologically this means that every part of man—mind, spirit, will, body—every part was affected by sin. The Puritans would further emphasize that not only does sin affect all of man, but also that sinfulness was significant. The practical result of this was the Puritan emphasis on the necessity to rear children correctly. The Puritans held a very high view of the family, with a stress on covenant relationships. This is part of the reason that Reformed theology is frequently called by the name "covenant theology."

The fourth principle of the Puritans was the purity of the church. It was this principle that gave them their name. Purity of the church meant that only true Christians should be in the church—not just anyone who wanted to join.

It also meant that worship forms of the church must be purely scriptural, not just the preaching, but also the music, the content of worship, everything. They denied the use of images in worship such as stained glass pictures, crucifixes and the like. This was the working out of Zwingli's Regulative Principle to its fullest extent. And, this meant that there were no hymns sung in Puritan churches—only the unaccompanied singing of metrical Psalms.

The main problem with the Puritans (and the place where they break with the principles of Sphere Sovereignty) is that they wanted to have the Church control the State. They did not see the validity of complete separation of Church and State. They simply wanted to reverse the situation in England where the State controlled the Church, and have it that the Church controlled the State.

At the end of the day in America, the decision was made that neither group should have control of the other—that there should be two separate spheres that should not be mixed—but that is not what the Puritans wanted. (We see a resurgence of this Puritan principle today in what is known as Theonomic Reconstructionism.)

By 1642, there was so much disruption between the people (represented by the Parliament) and the King of England that a civil war broke out. Oliver Cromwell was a young, obscure member of Parliament when the civil wars started. He was a minor member of the gentry (landowners who lived primarily from rental income.) When the supporters of the Parliament in its efforts to wrest control of the government from the King began to take military action, Cromwell became a Captain in that army.

Eight years later—after several significant battles (including fighting back invasions from armies loyal to the Scottish royal class) Cromwell was named the head of the army and, after the capture and execution of King Charles—became the head of state in England (although he refused an offer to become king).

During the early period of England's Civil War, the parliament—in loyalty to the people rather than the King, called an assembly of churchmen to meet to draw up principles of the true church. The Parliament did not want to maintain the Anglican Church—it wanted to have a truly Reformed church. The assembly was made up of 121 appointed members—

although the average attendance on any given day was between sixty and eighty. The members were primarily Puritans and Presbyterians. Four of the Anglican bishops were named as members, although is it not clear than any of them ever attended. The Church of Scotland sent six representatives.

The five principle accomplishments of the Westminster Assembly were, first of all, the adoption of a Presbyterian form of government. This was already in practice in Scotland, but only briefly came into practice in England. Cromwell did not want to upset his political compromise which kept him in power. So even though the Parliament voted to set up a Presbyterian church for England, Cromwell stopped it.

Second, they adopted a Directory of Public Worship. It was designed to replace the Anglican Book of Common Prayer. After Cromwell's death and the return of a King to power in England, this directory was set aside and not used again in the Anglican churches.

Third was the primary work of a detailed Confession of Faith. Although this document never became the doctrinal standard for the Church of England, it was adopted by the Church of Scotland and many other Reformed bodies over the centuries—including the PCA. In its original form, despite opposition from the Puritans, the Confession continued to maintain State control over the Church, but this has since been dropped by every Church which uses the Confession.

The fourth major accomplishment was the Larger Catechism. This document itself was debated for over a year. It was the strongest worded document adopted by the Assembly, and also the result of the strongest influence of the Puritans. It contains many issues that are still hotly debated in our day and age. The primary purpose of this document was for the training of church officers. (Try to picture a Scottish farmer walking behind his plow, reciting the words of the Larger Catechism!)

After the Assembly had finished its work and reported back to Parliament, they were instructed to add a fifth project—the Shorter Catechism. This was to be used in the training of children in the church. It was largely the work of one committee, and was developed as a reduction of the Larger Catechism—and as such it leaves out much that is included in the Confession of Faith.

The Westminster Assembly's Confession of Faith may be safely deemed the most perfect statement of Systematic Theology ever framed by the Christian Church. In comparison to similar documents from the relatively same time period, the Westminster Confession of Faith stands far superior in thoroughness, thoughtfulness and literary quality. For example, here is a section from the first chapter on the Bible:

V. We may be moved and induced by the testimony of the church to an high and reverent esteem of the Holy Scripture. And the heavenliness of the matter, the efficacy of the doctrine, the majesty of the style, the consent of all the parts, the scope of the whole (which is, to give all glory to God), the full discovery it makes of the only way of man's salvation, the many other incomparable excellencies, and the entire perfection thereof, are arguments whereby it doth abundantly evidence itself to be the Word of God: yet notwithstanding, our full persuasion and assurance of the infallible truth and divine authority thereof, is from the inward work of the Holy Spirit bearing witness by and with the Word in our hearts.

The results of the Westminster Assembly, which met for a total of nearly five years, went far beyond its immediate effect. Since Cromwell was an Independent, he never fully supported the results of the Westminster Assembly and it was used little in England at first. Within ten years, it had disappeared entirely. The Church of England remains—even still today—less reformed than any church among those we would consider Protestant.

## Chapter Eight
## The Law and the Prince – The Scottish Covenanters

We return now to zero in our focus more directly on the historical roots of the Presbyterian Church in America by returning to Scotland. During the period of political upheaval in England, while the Westminster Confession of Faith was being written, Scotland was having its own troubles. Although the Church had followed for the most part the teachings of the Reformation and the Presbyterian form of church government instituted during the time of John Knox, their remained hostility at the throne—especially during the reign of Charles I, who was from the Stuart line of kings and queens which had produced Mary, Queen of Scots.

Charles I had attempted to unite the Church of England and Scotland. Like his parents and grandparents, he had strong ties with France and had himself, married a French girl with royal blood. Through political maneuvering, he was attempting to have control over both the Church of Scotland and the Church of England and, had he been able to accomplish this, he would have moved them both back closer to Rome.

Under his direction, he had a common prayer book written to provide for similar worship services in both England and Scotland. While it wasn't all that much change for the Church of England, it was an enormous change in Scotland from the simplicity of the Reformed worship Knox had introduced. Thus, the people rebelled.

There is a great story about a woman who was a member of the church where Knox had pastored for several decades—St. Giles in Edinburgh. Her name was Genny Geddes. At the worship service where the new senior minister—who now, fitting into an Episcopalian hierarchal system, was known as a Dean—was seeking to introduce the new prayer book, Genny picked up a stool she was using as her seat and threw it up on the platform, striking the very pompous and richly robed clergyman with a blow to his body. Needless to say, a small riot broke out in the congregation that day.

As the opposition to the prayer book grew, a number of ministers and like-minded key political leaders gathered in 1638 to draft what they called a National Covenant. (The text is printed in Appendix A at the rear of the book.) The document was primarily theological, based on the teachings of the Swiss Reformation under Calvin. But it also spoke to the political independence of the Church from the laws of the State, which is to say, from control by the King. Six of the original signers of this National Covenant were invited to England to participate in the Westminster Assembly.

As an indication of how much the people opposed the changes being instituted in their churches, within two months virtually the entire population of Scotland—at least those not connected directly to the royal family—had signed the Covenant. Remembering the days not too long previous under Knox, an army of more than 30,000 men was ready to go to war if the ongoing battle of words turned into a battle of swords. It was quite clear that the Scots wanted no part of the Church of Rome.

This all was occurring just when the English Civil War had broken out and Oliver Cromwell had taken control of the government, having his own parliament elected. This caused some problems concerning the political allegiance of the Scots. At first the Covenanters (as those who signed this National Covenant had become known) were loyal to the new Parliament, and especially to the common people who had helped them win some great victories. But in a short period of time, in a very strange and not easily understood change of heart, some of the Scots shifted their support to the King. Remember—the King who had been overthrown in England was Charles I, and was in the Stuart line (from Scotland).

When Charles I was removed by Cromwell, he was succeeded by his son, Charles II. But he was for the first eleven years of his reign recognized as King only in Scotland. At the beginning of his reign, the Presbyterians in Scotland, as well as the Puritans in England, were faring quite well without interference from the State. But we must be reminded that Charles II, like his father, came from the Stuart line—and as you may recall from your high school history—it was the Stuart line that first proposed the doctrine of Divine Right—that it was God's will that there should be kings to rule on earth—and so this line of kings had the Divine Right to reign over the people.

You will also recall that the Scots were always loyal to their King, so the move to allow Charles II to come to the throne in Scotland was no big surprise—not that there wasn't opposition. Some of the gentry, led by the Marquis of Argyle, who was a staunch Presbyterian, knew that the whole Stuart family was Catholic, or at the very least, very pro-Catholic. Because the Church was so strong at the time, Charles II was very limited in his rule, particularly in matters of religion and other laws that were affected by religion.

Among those whose influence was very strong during this period in Scotland was a man named Samuel Rutherford. In 1627, he earned an M.A. from Edinburgh College, where he was appointed Professor of Humanity. He also served as the pastor of the church in Anwoth. He was one of the six Scots to work on the Westminster Confession of Faith. He was the author of a book entitled *Lex Rex,* which will become important to understand shortly.

After Cromwell died in 1658, Charles II assumed the English throne as well, in 1660. Naturally, this allowed him to grow in political power, even in Scotland. He had the military strength now to overthrow those who had been opposed to him earlier. The Earl of Argyll, the most prominent political leader who opposed the English throne, was condemned as a traitor and executed. Rutherford was also condemned, but he died of natural causes before the execution could be carried out.

Within a year of assuming the English throne, Charles II had a law passed called the Act Rescissory. It decreed that any minister who had been ordained since 1649 (under the rule of Presbyterians) must receive a "presentation" from the patron of his parish (remember these religious jobs were still controlled by local landowners) and *also* needed a "collation" from the bishop—both of these being requirements of the Church of England (or Anglican Church as it was now known). This law forced the Church of Scotland to return to Anglican forms of worship and government. Ministers who did not comply would lose their churches, their manses (this is the Scottish word that is equivalent to parsonages), their salary, and must move beyond the bounds of their presbyteries. Much to the surprise of Charles II, 250 Presbyterian pastors in Scotland refused to honor those terms.

What resulted would later cause John Wesley to comment concerning Charles II, "Oh, what a blessed Governor was that good-natured man, so-called King Charles the Second! Bloody Queen Mary was a lamb, a mere dove, in comparison to him!" Clearly, things did not go well under Charles II—in fact, persecution was rampant.

By 1663, the ministers who had been forced out of their churches began meeting out-of-doors, by necessity. Their meetings were called Conventicles—a word which means literally "to meet out of doors." Anyone caught attending one of these meetings was subject to terrible persecution.

Through some not totally understood military and political decisions in England to withdraw two of their generals from Scotland, there was a three-year period from (1669-1672) when the persecution let up considerably. This period has been known in Scottish Church history as The Blink (which, by the way, is the topic of my favorite question on the floor of Presbytery meetings to fluster young men standing their church history examinations for ordination!)

During The Blink, King Charles relented somewhat and offered two separate "indulgences" (not a great word to use concerning actions in Protestant churches—is it?) These were guarantees that any minister who had lost his church since the Act Rescissory had been passed in 1662 could return to the official ministry of the Church of Scotland—with full standing—merely by recognizing Charles II as the head of the Church.

This brought a split in the Covenanters. Some went along with the guarantee, returned to their churches and promised allegiance to Charles II as head of the Church. This "indulged" group reconstituted the Church of Scotland. Others refused and stayed outside the formal church. They were known as the "non-indulged" and their Church become known ultimately as the Reformed Presbyterians. Remember that name—it will appear again many times in this book.

The key question being discussed during this period was this: Can we any longer as Christians and freemen own (i.e., submit to) the authority, even in civil things, of a king who has violated so flagrantly his coronation oath? Had not the king forfeited all claim upon our allegiance, and by his reckless violation of the essential conditions of the social compact, set us free? The key answer to this question was found in a book that had been written several decades earlier, but only now grew into widespread understanding and reading. The book was Samuel Rutherford's *Lex Rex*.

The full title for the book, written in 1644, was *The Law and the Prince—a Dispute for the Just Prerogative of King and People*. It was written in response to those who held to the concept of Divine Right of a sovereign to rule and to demand an absolute and passive obedience of the subject (citizen) to the will of the sovereign (civil authority). Rutherford's response to this claim in his book became a call to what looked very much like a "Holy War" in Scotland in the 17th Century.

This issue is not simply a historical anecdote. There are Christians yet today who believe they must give total allegiance to the government because God's word requires rendering to Caesar what is Caesar's.

The real issue at stake is this. Which takes primacy—the law or the king? In this question, one is not to think of the king (or queen) as an individual person, but rather as the governing office holder. Rutherford taught that ultimately, the authority of the king rests in the hands of the people—who have the right to choose to give or not to give allegiance to the king. Based on this theory, it then becomes lawful for the people to recall powers from a king who does not rule according to law. Rutherford acknowledged that people are to suffer much before retaking power from a king. He also taught the king was responsible to defend the true (biblical) religion. But the key to Rutherford's word was that the "law" in view was to be God's law. Or, if it were a civil law, it was be a civil law based on biblical law.

The document itself was not an inspiring one to read. It was 600 pages of very heavy, even pedantic teaching. One commentator said it had "as much emotion as the multiplication tables." Nevertheless, it became a very important written document for the times.

This importance went beyond the borders of Scotland. John Witherspoon, a Presbyterian of Covenanter background, was the only minister to sign the Declaration of Independence in America and it is easy to see from his writings that he was influenced by Lex Rex. It was partly Lex Rex that led our nation's founders to believe that their actions at that time were not treasons but actually behaviors sanctioned by God's word.

In fact, Thomas Jefferson, who by any measure could best be defined as a deist and who was primarily influenced by the works of political philosopher John Locke, purposefully took the essential teachings of Lex Rex and secularized them (took them out of the religious realm).

The concepts of Lex Rex became the rallying cry for the non-indulged Covenanters and in May of 1679 a group of about eighty gather at Rutherglen, a town not far from

Glasgow, to disrupt a celebration of the restoration of many indulged clergy. They burned copies of all the acts of Parliament, which had brought back Episcopal forms to the Church of Scotland, and copies of all writings they could find opposed to the Reformation. This quickly brought to the attention of King Charles II what is known as the Second Revolt.

Described by some as resembling Judas Iscariot and by others as Emperor Julian the apostate, a nobleman named John Graham of Claverhouse had become the King's key general. Known simply as Claverhouse, he set the chief aim in his life as the full and complete defeat of the Covenanters and was known throughout Scotland as the Despot's Champion.

Having been unable to overcome the Covenanters in several small scrimmages in the early months of the Second Revolt, Claverhouse gathered the finest army available in Scotland and England and met the assembled non-indulged forces at the town of Bothwell Bridge. In a stunning defeat, more than 1,200 Covenanters were taken prisoner and kept without shelter for three months in the fall of the year.

Two of their ministers were hanged. Five were executed after being tried for the murder of a Scottish Archbishop several months earlier, although they were not the men involved in the murder, which was carried out by a band of radicals repudiated by the Covenanters. Hundreds of other prisoners were loaded on a ship to be carried to the Barbados Islands. Only fifty of those survived the storm and trouble-laden trip to become plantation slaves. It was clear that persecution was to be an understated word to describe how Claverhouse and the King would treat the rebellious Presbyterians.

# The Law and the Prince

After the great defeat at Bothwell Bridge, the non-indulged Reformed Presbyterians were forced underground. Three of the un-captured leaders (still recognizing that the underlying problem was that of constitutional issues faced by the English people though the reign of the Stuart lines of kings) decided to write down their views of constitutional government and through that, to seek to gain support. In the original draft of their document, there were three main points (in which you can see the influence of *Lex Rex*).

1.    The king was to be disowned for having rejected God.

2.    The monarchy was to be repudiated, as it was certain to lead to tyranny.

3.    A government according to biblical standards was to be set up.

While there is some historical dispute as to who really wrote this document, most historians credit it to the work of two Covenanter leaders, Henry Hall and Donald Cargill. The two men were traveling together the next summer (June of 1680) and were attacked by royal soldiers near the town of Queensferry. In the scuffle, Cargill escaped but Hall was killed. A scratch copy of the document on which they were working was found on Hall and preserved; it became known as the Queensferry Paper. A prize of 5,000 pounds was offered for the capture of Cargill.

This huge ransom brought Cargill to the attention of many people, and through him, the Queensferry Paper became famous. The other of the three initial leaders of the movement, a man named Richard Cameron, chose to publicize the matter rather dramatically. In a more brief form, he restated the same views that Hall and Cargill had expressed in the Queensferry

Paper, and then, with twenty other men, solemnly entered the market place in the town of Sanquhar. After singing a psalm and offering prayer, they posted it there for all to read. The posting of this Sanquhar Declaration was a bold, open act—displayed for everyone to see—and to the king's mind, constituted treason. (Appendix B contains details on the content of both the Queensferry Paper and the Sanquhar Declaration.) There was no longer any question. The battle was clearly a case of constitutional government against a despotic monarchy—a case of Calvinism against Catholicism.

Cargill was a much older man than Cameron, and undoubtedly looked on the younger man as his successor to Reformed Presbyterian leadership. Both men were properly educated ministers and beloved by the Scots. As the only two remaining Covenanter pastors in Scotland, their parishes were not small.

Traveling by night, hiding in the boggy moors by day, ministering to the faithful, encouraging the weak and suffering, and consistently upholding the doctrine of the Lordship of Christ over his Church, these two men faced a task scarcely equaled in any day or age. Cameron, known for his daring act at Sanquhar, was also known for his gentleness of spirit, his kind heart and his love. His preaching filled the hearts of the spiritually hungry, faithful believers throughout Scotland.

Shortly after the Sanquhar incident, Cargill and Cameron enjoyed one of their rare meetings, and on a Sunday, Cameron preached from the text, *"Be still and know that I am God."* Little did they know it was their last Sabbath together. During the following week, Cameron and several other men who were traveling had stopped to rest at a bleak stretch of mossy ground. Here they were discovered by the King's army and within a few moments, nine of the Covenanters were dead—including Richard Cameron. One of the soldiers cut off his head and hands and carried them to Edinburgh for the promised reward.

This victorious soldier paid tribute to his fallen foe as he handed over the body parts to the King's council. Patrick Walker, in his book *Six Saints of the Covenant* published in London in 1901, records the soldier's words for posterity, "There are the head and hands of a man who lived praying and preaching, and died praying and fighting."

For some bizarre reason, the body parts were then carried to a nearby prison to be given to Cameron's aged father. When asked if he recognized them, he picked them up, kissed them and said (recorded also by Walker), "I know them. I know them. They are my son's, my dear son's. It is the Lord, good is the will of the Lord, who cannot wrong me nor mine, but has made goodness and mercy to follow us all our days."

Donald Cargill did not last much longer. Walker tells us that about a year later, he preached, exhorting "us all earnestly to dwell in the clefts of the Rock, to hide ourselves in the wounds of Christ, and to wrap ourselves in the believing application of the promises flowing therefrom, thus to make our refuge under the shadow of His wings, until these sad calamities pass over, and the Dove comes back with the olive branch in her mouth." The following morning he was captured, and when he climbed the scaffold to his execution, he said, "God knows I go up this ladder with less fear, confusion or perturbation of mind, than ever I entered a pulpit to preach."

For two years the Covenanters, or rather the Cameronians, as they were now called, persisted without a minister. But a young man named James Renwick, who had witnessed Cargill's execution, completed his theological studies in Holland and returned to Scotland in 1683. The following year a group of Anglicans asked the Cameronians to help with an effort to overthrow the government. The Scottish reply—that they were willing to help overthrow tyranny but could have no association with Anglicans—was discovered when its bearer was arrested. The new wave of persecution which broke out as a result of this note became known as the Killing Time and spanned the last year of Charles II's reign and nearly all of James II's reign.

James II, the brother of Charles II, ruled from 1685 to 1688. He made it clear that there would be no rest in the kingdom until all of southern and western Scotland was turned into a hunting ground. Bloodhounds were released in order to lead the royal soldiers more accurately to Cameronian homes, field meetings, and hiding places. Death came in a variety of forms during the Killing Time—including execution, imprisonment for life, exile, drowning and starvation.

One of the most famous and touching stories is that of two women named Margaret—an elderly widow and an eighteen year old girl. They were tied to stakes on the beach at Solway Firth so that as the tide came in, the young girl saw the older woman drown, while the persecutors nearby taunted her to renounce her faith. Neither woman recanted, but bravely met their ugly death. Such stories were numerous.

Another extract comes from Walker's biography cited earlier. "Andrew Hislop, a lad of seventeen, son of a widow in Annandale, was condemned to death for helping his mother care for a dying Covenanter and then bury him after he had died—a man whose name they did not even know. "I can look my death bringers in the face without fear," said the boy stoutly, "and I have nothing to be ashamed of...." After his execution, the house of his mother, who had somehow eluded them, was striped of all its possession and then razed to the ground.

By 1688, an estimated 18,000 Reformed Presbyterians had been killed or exiled. Historians generally wish to overlook Charles II's treatment of the Covenanters by saying that he was less barbaric to the people he murdered than the French government was to the people it murdered.

Anyway, back to Renwick. He was described in temperament as a combination of John Knox and David Brainerd—sharing their fearless courage toward men and their trembling awe of God. For five years, the Cameronians fed on the spiritual meat imparted to them by Renwick, their only minister. And by 1688, the Killing Time was nearly over. James II had overplayed his hand and was forced to flee to France when he was faced by an unfriendly Parliament in England, which was determined to place a Protestant monarch on the British throne. But before this could take place, the bloodthirsty Stuart persecution had to claim one more victim.

The era of persecution had been ushered in by the execution in 1661 of the Marquis of Argyle and was to be closed by the execution of James Renwick. In February 1688, Renwick was captured in Edinburgh and turned over to the city guard. Looking at the youthful twenty-six year old, the astonished guard captain exclaimed (according to Walker), "What! Is this boy that Mr. Renwick whom the nation has been so troubled with?" On the scaffold, Renwick sang the 103rd Psalm, read the 19th Chapter of Revelation and prayed. A friend wrote of him (again recorded by Walker), "When I speak of him as a man, none more comely in features, none more prudent, none more heroic in spirit, yet none more meek, more humane, and condescending…He learned the truth and counted the cost, and so sealed it with his blood."

When James II was run out of the country, his Protestant daughter named Mary Stuart, was living in Holland with her husband, William of Orange. William, born in 1650, was the son of William, Prince of Orange, and the elder Mary Stuart (daughter of Charles I). Thus husband and wife were also first cousins, both being a grandchild of Charles I. The young couple, evermore known as William and Mary, were offered the unprecedented position of joint sovereigns by the British Parliament, and the young couple came to England—and a new era began. The struggle of Parliament against an arbitrary monarch had finally culminated in a constitutional monarchy.

The unfair taxes of James I, the betrayal of the Right of Petition by Charles I, Charles I's eleven years of despotism, the religious atrocities of Charles II and James II, were all past now. Parliament could force a king to flee, and Parliament could invite the king it chose. Parliament controlled the fiscal policy, and Parliament controlled the law. Absolutionism would reign in France for another century and be overthrown in a gory revolution. But constitutionalism mounted the throne of England and Scotland in 1688 with scarcely a murmur—but twenty-seven years of the shed blood of the Covenanters had preceded it.

It is extremely significant that the government changes accomplished in 1688 fulfilled, to a very large extent, the request of Cargill in the Queensferry Paper and Cameron in the Sanquhar Declaration. They were, so to speak, eight years ahead of their time.

Perhaps we Americans should say that they were a century ahead of their time, not only in their requests but in the fact that the very wording of our Declaration of Independence bears striking resemblance to these Covenanter political documents, which were truly the first of their kind. The Covenanters left a political inheritance which not only their spiritual heirs have enjoyed, but all other people of the free world as well.

The relief that accompanied William and Mary's accession to the throne is immeasurable. They were not anti-Presbyterian, and many favorable actions were taken in Scotland's behalf. Under their leadership, laws were made against the Pope and for the maintenance of the Reformed faith. The Westminster Confession was adopted, Presbyterian Church government and discipline were established, patronage was finally abolished and the 1$^{st}$ General Assembly of the Church of Scotland was appointed to meet.

With such an arrangement, one might expect the weary Cameronians to have accepted it all without dispute, but there were, nevertheless, serious defects in the settlement brought by William and Mary. The two worst were the failure to revoke the Act of Rescission of 1661 that started the whole problem. The second main objection was the retention by the King of his headship over the Scottish Church. To the strictest among the Reformed Presbyterians, Christ, and no one else, was head of the Church. They could not participate in the General Assembly and so there always remained separate and apart from the Church of Scotland a group known as Covenanters or Reformed Presbyterians. Some of them moved to Ireland. Some to South Africa, and some of them came to America.

Most of the RP's (to use today's acronym) settled either in Pennsylvania or in Mecklenburg County, North Carolina. A year before the Declaration of Independence was drawn up by Jefferson, the Mecklenburg Reformed Presbyterians adopted a similar declaration, much of which includes the same phrases and ideas that Jefferson used in his Declaration.

The Covenanters in the United States remain a separate church even to this day (although it is very small). They still practice exclusive psalmody in their churches and one cannot be a member without signing the Covenant and ascribing to the Westminster Standards. We will see another group of these RP's later on in this work when we deal with 20th Century history.

## Chapter Nine
## The Lighthouse on the Hill – Puritans Come to America

The first 100 years of church history in America were primarily about the Puritans and their heirs, who formed both Congregational and Baptist churches. The title of this chapter, you will notice, is "The Lighthouse on the Hill". This title is taken from the historical understanding of the purpose of the Puritan experiment in America—their desire to establish a biblically based "lighthouse" on the "hill" of America.

The Puritans envisioned a time when the Church would—by design—be made up of visible saints only, when church discipline would be strictly practiced. And, only when those members were in good standing in the church, could they take part in civil government. The Puritans had tried to press this in England, but failed. So they came to America to purposefully seek to set up their idea of that combination of nation and church. We frequently forget that the Mayflower compact was in fact a religious covenant that these people made with their God. The whole reason behind the settlement of the Massachusetts Bay Colony was religious motivation.

The main immigration of Puritans took place in 1630. The first governor of Massachusetts was a layman named John Winthrop. And interestingly enough, while the Puritans still considered themselves to be a part of the Church of England, they set up a totally different form of church government—what we today call Congregationalism. In this form of government the vote of the congregation decides all issues—membership, form, order, building, officers, discipline, budget—everything.

While the Puritans had not planned this form of church government, their separation from the Church of England and the vary nature of the environment in which they found themselves—with so many problems and decisions to be made—forced the people to band closely together. There were no strong natural leaders among them, no one dominating force as you would expect in an Episcopal form of government. So, Congregationalism came to America. And in fact, it still dominates America, not so much because of biblical principle (I discuss this at length in a separate book entitled *Biblical Church Government*), but for very pragmatic reasons.

Remember, the Massachusetts Bay Colony was a Calvinistic church in which the Church controlled the State. One had to be a church member in order to vote in public elections. So the church meetings became town meetings. This form of town meeting set the tone in the colonies for the civil governments to follow—even when they were free of Church control.

By the second generation, there was a reduction of zeal and change in the values of the people. A compromise allowed the baptism of children of parents who were not active church members—and very likely not even Christians. This was known as the Half-Way Covenant. By the third generation, all this zeal the Puritans had brought with them for purity in the Church was lost.

The first break from this strong hand of church government over the state was led by Roger Williams, the founder of Rhode Island—which was the first colony to allow for total freedom of worship. This became the American way for the church for the rest of our history. While Williams' followers were the first to practice immersion, it was essentially the issue of Church and State separation that brought about this division among the Puritans.

The most influential religious leaders of this next period of history were two Congregational ministers, a father and son. A man named Increase Mather was the pastor of Second Congregational Church in Boston. His son, Cotton Mather, was his associate pastor, and at a very young age, took over the full-time preaching in the church. Cotton Mather held to all the same theology as the Puritans. He preached the word of God faithfully, as did any of the preceding generation, but things were different.

Other clergy gave that particular vocation a bad name by getting involved in the witchcraft trials in Salem, rather than simply preaching the word of God. The merchants began to doubt whether the Bible really supported their newly found ideas of commerce and amassing wealth.

On the educational front, Harvard University, which had been founded as a Christian college (Increase Mather had served as President when his son took over the preaching at Second Church) began to teach classes other than Bible and divinity More and more students wanted to study business, the arts and sciences, and forgo any religious studies at all.

So the Mathers and their friends moved down to Connecticut to start another great Christian college—they called that one Yale! (Oh, you didn't know that Harvard and Yale were once Christian colleges? I wonder why not.) Anyway, Cotton Mather wrote a two volume history of the Plymouth Colony that had gone before him. In his summary paragraph, this is what he wrote, "Religion brought forth prosperity, and the daughter destroyed the mother."

Dwell on that thought just a bit. "Religion" of course is the Puritan experiment. The people gave up homes, family and security in England and the Netherlands, and paid the price for moving to a barren new world to start over with religious liberty. With the freedom to live their lives according to the word of God, this religion 'brought forth prosperity. In other words, the Massachusetts Bay Colony had grown and expanded, and formed new colonies in Connecticut, Rhode Island and New York. People had jobs, raised children, started colleges and enjoyed prosperity.

Back to Cotton Mather's summary. "Religion brought forth prosperity, and the daughter destroyed the mother." The daughter, of course, was prosperity and the mother was religion. So what is it that Cotton Mather was saying? Let's replace his sentence with the synonyms. "Prosperity destroyed religion."

In just the third full generation in America, prosperity destroyed religion. Some might say it didn't really destroy it—it just changed it a little. But, listen to what one of Cotton Mather's biographers had to say about this period. He was speaking of Mather's preaching ministry to the large, wealthy congregation at Second Church, Boston. (Remember, Cotton Mather was the greatest preacher of his time.) "Mather preached, but no one listened."

You see it is possible for the truth of the word of God to be preached, and for no one to listen. For no one to understand its implications for their own lives. For no one to apply those principles to their lives. For no one to change their lives according to what they hear in the word of God. By the way, the name of that astute biographer was Ben Franklin. The full quote has one more phrase, "Mather preached, but no one listened. But Mather just kept preaching!"

So the key issue in the church at the turn of the 18$^{th}$ Century was not Justification by Faith as it had been at the time of the Reformation, but rather morality. (Does that sound at all familiar to you today?) The central belief in churches of this period was that what really mattered in order to be a good person, even a good Christian person, was to have good outward morals—and for society to have good outward morals.

Into this situation, in Northampton, Massachusetts, in the 1720s a preacher named Solomon Stoddard began to preach the great Reformation themes of repentance and faith. His was a lone voice for the true faith in New England. Then, in the fullness of time, came the man of God for this period of history—Jonathan Edwards.

Edwards, who lived from 1703 to 1758, was the greatest mind of this time. Some say (and I tend to agree) that he was the greatest mind to ever have lived in North America.

He was raised in a large Massachusetts family. As a young man, he became interested in science and went to Yale to study science. He even remained there for a brief period to serve as a tutor. While at college, he was converted at a gospel meeting at which a fellow student was speaking on the topic of the Sovereignty of God. He began immediately to keep a diary of his life, but kept it in secret code, which has just been broken in the last few decades.

He married an equally brilliant Christian girl in 1727 and joined his Grandfather, Solomon Stoddard, as Associate

Pastor of his church in Northampton. In 1731, he was invited to preach at a Harvard graduation. There he reasserted the basic tenants of Calvinism that for nearly 100 years had been neglected in New England. He was not invited back to Harvard again.

In 1734, Edwards had become pastor of the church in Northampton when Stoddard had died, and he began preaching regularly on Justification by Faith, one of the main tenets of the Reformation, but a long neglected theme in New England. It was during this period that he preached his sermon with the well-known title, "Sinners in the Hands of an Angry God."

Under his preaching a true, God-given revival (we will talk about man-made revivals in a later chapter) began in his own church. By 1735, 300 people had been converted and the revival began to spread throughout the region. In 1740, George Whitefield visited Northampton, and revival broke out again. For the next ten years, there was a great revival throughout New England—basically as a result of Whitefield's and Edward's work. The period is known in our history as the Great Awakening; it paralleled a similar revival in England brought about through the preaching of Whitefield and the Wesleys.

In 1750, Edwards was asked to leave his pulpit because of an issue concerning church discipline brought up at a congregational meeting where Edwards called out by name several teenagers he accused of improper behavior. He spent eight years as a missionary to the Indians in Western Massachusetts and New York. In 1758, he became the president of a new Calvinistic Presbyterian founded college—

the College of New Jersey (later to be known as Princeton University). He died that same year.

We want to take a brief excursus at this point to learn more about George Whitefield, an Anglican, and about John and Charles Wesley, also Anglicans who founded the Methodist Church. Their history is so deeply intertwined into the history of the Great Awakening we must be aware of at least a brief outline of what happened.

John Wesley was born in the same year as Jonathan Edwards (1703) but lived much longer (1791). His father was an Anglican minister who, with his wife Susanna, raised nineteen children. (Reading the biography of Susanna Wesley is definitely required for any woman who might find herself married to a minister!)

While they were students at Oxford, John and his brother, Charles, formed "Holy Clubs" which focused on the moral necessity of being a good person (exactly the same emphasis we saw in America during this period). During this period both young men struggled with a lack of assurance of salvation and sought to develop sufficient piety to feel saved. This experience would later greatly affect their theological understandings. They both took ordination as Anglican priests, following in their father's footsteps.

John and Charles then decided to become missionaries to Native Americans in Georgia—in the area near what we know today as Savannah. Charles lasted about six months; John just a year longer. They were not at all popular with other settlers. They were very polished and "slick" and sought to implement their high church Anglicanism even among the Native Americans.

John went through a disastrous romance during this period. He fell in love with the daughter of a prominent settler, but she suddenly and unexpectedly dumped him and married someone else (most likely on the advice of her father who was not a supporter of the Wesleys). Apparently, John had a personal altercation with the young lady's new husband; the bailiff's records show John Wesley was arrested during this period.

On the Trans-Atlantic trip to Georgia, the Wesleys had met some Moravians, a pietist group similar to the Swiss Brethren. They held to strong views of extreme piety and a simple life style. Wesley's journals tell of the calmness the Moravians exhibited during very severe storms at sea when Wesley thought the ship would sink.

After his return to England, John was again influenced by the Moravians; he began to study their views of piety and sanctification. At the same time, Charles took ill and nearly died. His recovery seemed almost miraculous and resulted in his own conversion.

Three days later, John was attending a prayer meeting during which the speaker told of Luther's conversion experience. Let me read an except from William P. Barker's *Who's Who In Church History* (Old Tappen, NJ: Fleming H. Revell, 1969), page 299:

> On May 24, 1738, John Wesley reluctantly attended an Anglican "society" in Aldersgate Street, London. Wesley dated his rebirth from that evening. Listening to a reading of Luther's preface to the Commentary on the

Epistle to the Romans, Wesley felt his "heart strangely warmed." He exultantly described the experience: "While he was describing the change which God works in the heart through faith in Christ, I felt...I did trust in Christ, Christ alone for my salvation; and an assurance was given me that he had taken away my sins, even mine and saved me from the law of sin and death"

John and Charles began reading Puritan literature and immediately reacted against the coldness and apparent lack of conversion among most Anglicans. The met George Whitefield, another enthusiastic, clearly converted Anglican priest. They began forming their own societies and preaching throughout England. Theirs was open field preaching (they were seldom invited by Anglican clergy to preach in their churches).

The ministry of the Wesleys and Whitefield resulted in what became known as the Evangelical Awakening in England. The preaching frequently resulted in enthusiasm and emotional results such as fainting, shrieks and hysteria. The Anglicans were horrified by this and attacked the Wesleys, ridiculing their procedures.

Although they considered themselves to be loyal Anglicans, they organized new converts into groups which they called classes. John Wesley originally intended these to be an order within the established church. Ultimately, they would put classes together into a "society" and erected a chapel for one of the societies in Bristol, and later for one in London.

These societies had their own ministers who were not trained nor ordained as Anglican clergy. As such, they could not serve communion. Wesley finally agreed to ordain these men himself—even though he was not a bishop (which was a requirement for one to have the authority to do ordination services).

The Methodist church grew from these societies. They developed the concept of circuit riders who would travel from one place to another to minister, rather than living in just one town. They ultimately appointed superintendents to hold the groups of societies together. The name Methodist came from the methods practiced by Wesley and his followers; they were different from the traditional Anglican methods.

The Evangelical Awakening had a long-term effect, by developing a social conscience in England. The Methodists were also credited with initiating Sunday schools, which were formed to bring street children in on Sunday afternoons to teach them how to read and write and never were intended for the purpose of Christian education of children, or even adults.

George Whitefield—who was a prominent member of the leadership group among the Methodists—was born in northern England in 1714 (which makes him eleven years younger than John Wesley and Jonathan Edwards). His father was an innkeeper, a heavy drinker and carouser who remained poor all his life. He died when George was very young to leave his impoverished mother to raise the children.

George had a wild childhood, but was brilliant in school. His conversion took place over a long process during his adolescence. He was converted earlier than the Wesleys as a result of a spiritual crisis in his life, simply reading the Bible. Finally, his mother remarried and could afford to send him to college. He went to Oxford on a scholarship and there joined the "Holy Club." He ultimately changed his program of study and was ordained as an Anglican priest.

After the Wesleys returned from Georgia, Whitefield joined them. He decided not to pursue a normal pastorate; he was the first of the group to experiment with open-air preaching. He had a strong, clear voice and was able to preach (actually involved in public speaking) from forty to sixty hours per week for thirty-four years. He preached long, detailed sermons with deep intellectual content.

Whitefield would not use altar calls or any form of an invitation system (that developed in the next century). He preached to more people than anyone in history—with the possible exception of Billy Graham (but only if you add in Billy's TV audiences).

Whitefield's theology was that of strict Calvinism which resulted in a disagreement with the Wesleys on several important points. Whitefield was convinced of the truth of Reformed theology, while Wesley's Moravian influence brought him to an Arminian position.

Wesley did not believe in total depravity. He felt election was conditioned on foreknowledge. He believed in a universal atonement. He felt that man could, in fact, resist the grace of God. And, (as his primary issue of difference with Calvinism) he did not believe that man could have definite assurance and therefore he did not believe in the perseverance of the saints. (Note all the points of the followers of Jacob Arminians and the Remonstrants at the Synod of Dordt.)

Wesley also believed in the ability of total sanctification in this life (perfectionism) and thus pressed for what later became known as the Holiness Movement. There are many denominations in America today—including nearly all the Pentecostal churches formed at the beginning of the 20th Century—that follow this holiness teaching.

Whitefield wanted to continue to work with the Wesleys despite their disagreements and at first they just agreed not to talk about their differences. However, Charles (John's brother) broke the treaty and began writing pamphlets opposing Calvinism. This broke the working relationship, although the three men remained personal friends throughout their lifetimes.

As an interesting aside, the real battle was not so much in pamphlets as it was in hymns—and was carried on in the writing of new hymns. Whitefield's primary protagonist was Augustus Toplady, author of "Rock of Ages." Just as was the case in the early centuries of the Christian Church, hymns were being used to teach people theology!

Whitefield remained in the Anglican church. He developed many friends and benefactors among Anglican circles— especially in the upper classes—and was able to reach this portion of society in a way the Wesleys never could.

Whitefield made seven trips to America. The first trip was to Georgia to establish an orphanage outside of Savannah (which is still operating today). On his second trip, he traveled north and met with two Presbyterian brothers named Tennent (more on that in the next chapter). On his third trip, he was invited by Jonathan Edwards to New England. He landed in Newport and preached there in an Anglican church. (I recall sitting in that same sanctuary in the early 1980s to hear the Archbishop of Canterbury preach.)

Whitefield remained in New England for six weeks and the revival that had begun in Northampton spread quickly throughout New England. The initial emotionalism at conversion quickly passed away and people actually got involved in local churches. This was a tremendous period of church growth and influence in society. There was a clear division between "converted" people who followed New England theology and "liberals" in the established congregational churches. (Harvard became truly liberal at this time, in reaction to the Great Awakening).

Whitefield made one later trip to New England and several others to Virginia and Georgia. On one trip, he was preaching in Charleston, SC and the Anglican clergy would not allow him to preach in their pulpits. He became extremely demoralized over this, and on his next trip to New England took ill and died.

There were some significant results brought about by the Great Awakening. There was a return to the stress on the seriousness of sin and the need for personal salvation. There was a return to the authority of the Scriptures in an age of science and reason. There was a return to the purity of the church in an age of growing tolerance. There was a new reaching of the masses and eventually the growth of world missions.

Although it was never the outward, stated purpose of the Great Awakening, many moral and social improvements came about in the society. An end came to the practice of dueling, people began to examine the practice of slavery and it was abolished in the north; sex and violence was reduced in the entertainment areas of sports and the theatre. What the moralistic preaching of the earlier generation could not bring about was achieved by the preaching of biblical doctrine. (This is a lesson that could certainly be learned and applied in our generation, isn't it?)

In a very real sense, the Great Awakening must be recognized as the second greatest God-given revival in the history of the Christian Church—only behind the Reformation.

## Chapter Ten
## From a Log House to the Ivy League –
## Presbyterians Come to America

**P**arallel to all of the history involving Congregationalists we discussed in the previous chapter, there is some Presbyterian history to be discussed—but not as much, in terms of numbers of people. The first Presbyterians did not arrive on the American shores until the second wave of immigration when the first Scots began to arrive. The first presbytery of those originally affiliated with the Church of Scotland formed in Philadelphia in 1706. (We will celebrate the 300$^{th}$ anniversary of that event next year).

There are various accounts of the makeup of this presbytery. The official history of the mainline Presbyterian Church in the United States of America indicates that eight Presbyterian ministers met and formed the Presbytery of Philadelphia. The leader of this group was Francis Makamie, educated in Scotland but ordained in Northern Ireland; he had arrived in America as a missionary in 1681. He bridged the gap well between divergent views among those with Scottish, Irish, and English roots who considered themselves to be Presbyterians.

Right from the beginning, however, we see tensions between the different groups—tensions which are still apparent yet today—in the area known as Subscription. Those with roots in Scotland felt all officers should be in complete accord with the Westminster standards, which were the doctrinal basis for the church. Those with ties to New England felt that allegiance to the authority of Scripture was enough, and this group at first held the power.

By 1729, the Synod of Philadelphia (a Synod is a group of presbyteries in a specific region) brought about some surface peace on this issue through an Adopting Act, which required subscription to the Westminster standards while allowing for differences (they referred to them as scruples) in areas of non-essential doctrines. However, the two groups remained at heart uncommitted to this compromise and since the final decisions in the case of ministers were left to the presbyteries, and to local churches in the case of ruling elders, the differences remained.

In the midst of this tension, a new group arose to prominence, led by William Tennent, Sr. and his three sons. Tennent had been ordained originally as an Episcopal priest in Ireland. He came to America in 1716 and married the daughter of a Presbyterian minister, and quickly joined the Presbyterian Church. He finally settled in eastern Pennsylvania and began teaching (using directed reading and tutoring) his three sons and other men interested in becoming ministers.

There was no Presbyterian seminary in America at that time and the other ministers, who felt that only official seminaries in the British Isles could provide valid training, objected to Tennent's "Log College" as they denigratingly referred to his school.

The timeframe for these events was parallel with the preaching of Stoddard and Edwards in New England and in many ways became the root of the Great Awakening in the Middle Colonies. Tennent taught the more conservative New England Puritan theology coupled with Presbyterian Church government. He stressed experiential (or experimental) religion, with a stress on the absolute need for a clear conversion experience.

Soon four young men completed their studies at the Log College and assumed their own pastorates in the region. One son, Gilbert Tennent, became a pastor in New Brunswick, New Jersey. He became close friends with a Dutch pastor in nearby Raritan who was also an evangelical. Gilbert began working extensively doing what we would call personal evangelism today, which resulted in many conversions—as far away as Staten Island near New York City.

His brother John became the pastor at Freehold, New Jersey and a quiet revival began there as well. John died suddenly, and the third brother, William Jr., took his place. Slowly the Great Awakening was taking root in the area. While the results were not as startling in terms of outward signs and effects as in New England, the validity of the conversions was evident by the growing numbers of people affected. This movement took on the name of the Revival Party within Presbyterian circles.

At the same time, there was a growing immigration from Ireland and these Presbyterians were much more traditional. At the next meeting of the Presbyterian Synod, the traditionalists won a vote requiring that all ministers must be trained at seminaries located at major universities (there were none in America at the time) or be subject to examination by the Synod (rather than by the more localized presbyteries). This was a direct blow to the Log College.

Into this midst arrives George Whitefield in late 1739 and early 1740. Since Whitefield was seldom invited to preach in Anglican churches, he took advantage of opportunities offered by the Tennents and their friends. and it was mostly through Presbyterian churches that the revival spread through the Middle Colonies.

However, a division within the Presbyterians remained which almost defies understanding. History proved that both sides sought well-trained clergy and intellectual understanding of the historic doctrines, yet there seemed to be no way to bring harmony. Tennent and the New England theology group were one side; the Scots-Irish group was the other.

In the middle of this tension, Gilbert Tennent preached at a church in Nottingham, Pennsylvania—within the bounds of a Scots-Irish controlled presbytery—on the topic "The Dangers of an Unconverted Ministry" and the battle lines were drawn. The result was an action at the Synod of 1741 when a group of the Scots-Irish party drafted a protest against the actions of the Revival party. As more and more men went forward to sign this document, they discovered they had the majority of votes and quickly passed a motion declaring themselves to be the "true" Synod, thus throwing out the Log College men. This was, by all rules of parliamentary procedure at least, an illegal act—but it carried the day.

The two groups have become known in history as the Old Side (Scots-Irish, traditional) and New Side (Log College, New England theology). After several attempts at healing failed, the New Side formed the Synod of New York, with churches spread from New Hampshire through Virginia.

The evangelistic zeal of these New Side Presbyterians resulted in what historians refer to as a Second Awakening, which took place not only in the more populous areas but also in the frontier of the day. It was nowhere as complete or effective as the Great Awakening, but still significant enough to be recognized. This Second Awakening had three distinct groups, which are worth noting.

One was a Virginia group. Some laymen living near Fredericksburg, Virginia began studying the Bible and came under the influence of others of the New Side group. They decided to travel to the Virginia capital at Williamsburg to seek help in starting their own church. As they were traveling, they spent the night at an inn near Richmond. There in the attic they discovered a copy of the Westminster Confession of Faith and began reading it. By the time they had their interview with the Governor, the told him they wanted a church that taught this doctrine.

The Western Group was active mostly in Kentucky. Their course of growth was quite different, and since it became the beginning of what we will call the Modern Revivalism in a later chapter, we will save our examination of this group until then.

The original Eastern Group was the largest—resulting in the formation of the 1$^{st}$ General Assembly in 1789. Since Presbyterians have always made education one of their primary core values, the establishment of a college became a vision for the leadership of the New Side Presbyterians. It is important to notice that this first Presbyterian college was formed by the Revival Party, New-Side presbyteries.

Jonathan Dickinson, the leader of the New England New Side group, was selected to become the first President of the college and it was established in 1747 in Elizabethtown, New Jersey (close to New York as well as the Middle Colonies) where Dickinson was then serving as pastor. He was joined by another minister to serve as tutor and together, they began with ten students. However, within five months Dickinson died.

He was succeeded by another pastor named Aaron Burr (father of the more famous man bearing that name). Burr served for nearly ten years and provided the leadership needed to move the college to the town of Princeton, New Jersey and to the purchase of Nassau Hall, at the time the finest structure to house any school in America. After Burr's death, there was a quick succession of short-term presidents, all of whom died in office. Jonathan Edwards served one year; Samuel Davies served two years; Samuel Finley (a Log College leader) served about five years before his death. It was the election of Finley's successor as President of the College of New Jersey (as it was called in those days) who would make a major impact not only on Presbyterianism but also on America.

In 1758, the Old Side and New Side Presbyterians had negotiated a reunion. The Old Side not only had not grown, but had lost ministers and members, while the New Side had more than tripled the number of ministers in just fifteen years. So the settlement favored the New Side in every way—including the election of Gilbert Tennent as Moderator.

Gilbert had moved back in 1743 to the call as Pastor of Second Presbyterian in Philadelphia—a church built on the strength of Whitefield's preaching. Tennent became more moderate in his views during his term there and thus was able to provide leadership in the healing of the first of what would turn out to be many schisms among Presbyterians in America.

By the time came to elect the next President of the College of New Jersey, there had been more immigration by the Scots-Irish who would have leaned toward the Old Side positions. So, it became clear that the new President must be acceptable to both sides. The man who was chosen was not only that, but much more.

John Witherspoon was a leader in the Church of Scotland and was known there as both an evangelical and an intellectual. After two years of considering the call to come to the colonies, he arrived in Princeton in 1768 where he served for a quarter of a century. He served not only as a great leader in the Presbyterian Church but at the same time provided great political leadership. He instilled a Scots emphasis in a denomination that had been leaning very much towards New England congregationalism, and this led to the formation of a national General Assembly in 1789. He served in the

Continental Congress and was the one clergyman among the signers of the Declaration of Independence.

We must also understand that, parallel with this "mainline" Presbyterian history, there was slowly developing a separate history among Reformed Presbyterians. These were Christians in America whose background and tradition can be found in various groups in Scotland; they have been referred to at different times as Cameronians and Covenanters.

In 1732, a group of Reformed Presbyterians organized themselves into praying societies. These groups formed because they had no ordained men who agreed with their doctrinal position. They continued to prefer not joining in fellowship with others of the Church of Scotland background (the strain of the Covenanter persecutions remained for a long time). The first of these societies was led by a layman named Alexander Craighead.

Eventually a group of these praying societies met in a conference at the town of Middle Octarara, Pennsylvania in November of 1743. This group petitioned the Reformed Presbytery of Scotland to send ordained men to America to help in the work.

The first Reformed Presbyterian minister came from Scotland in 1752. He served alone among the Reformed Presbyterians for over twenty years. In 1774, two more ministers from Scotland arrived and the first official Presbytery of Reformed Presbyterians was formed at Paxtang, Pennsylvania on March 10, 1774.

Following in the trend of confederation which was abounding in the country at the time—and which became reflected in religious affairs throughout America—the Reformed Presbytery gave unanimous approval in December of 1781 to a basis of union between their Presbytery and a separate, but similar Presbytery—known as the Associate Presbytery.

In 1753, a group from what had become known as the Associate Synod of Scotland and Ireland, who had separated from the Church of Scotland at a time later than the Covenanters, formed their own presbytery in the Susquehanna Valley of Pennsylvania. This group would remain separate for several decades until their merger with the Reformed Presbyterians to form the Associate Reformed Synod in 1782.

The Associate Reformed Synod later merged with a branch of the Reformed Presbyterians and became known as the United Presbyterian Church. The UPC remained separate until it merged with the larger, mainline Presbyterians in 1958 to form the Presbyterian Church, USA. Since we are focusing in this volume on the historical roots of today's PCA, we will skip further examination of this particular group. We will also only mention the Associate Reformed Presbyterians that began as a separate denomination in the middle of the 19th Century and remain as an active and growing denomination today.

While the three ministers in the Reformed Paxtang Presbytery took part in the 1782 merger to form the Associate Reformed Synod, not all of their churches and people were willing to take part. Many Covenanters still objected to the "loose" theology of the merged church, particularly on such issues as exclusive psalmody, closed communion and ecumenism. It was their determination that a continuing Reformed presbytery testimony should remain in America.

It is interesting to note that—even at this early date—it is the laity who remained more conservative than their clergy. Finding themselves without ordained ministers, the Covenanters in America made application to the Reformed Presbytery of Scotland for assistance. In 1789, a minister came from Scotland to survey the work, but shortly thereafter returned to Scotland. In 1792 and 1793, two men were sent and together with a man who had been sent in 1790 from the Reformed Presbytery of Ireland, organized as a committee of the Scottish presbytery to oversee the affairs of the praying societies in America. This manner of oversight of the church in America proved to be unsatisfactory, since the actual governing body was so far away.

Eventually, a Presbytery was formed at Philadelphia in 1798 and the Covenanters - now using the name Reformed Presbyterians - were again able to ordain their own men. The amount of growth by 1809 ensured that the three areas with churches each became a separate presbytery and a synod was formed. With this came even more growth within the denomination.

One of the basic principles of the Covenanters was that they believed that the individual's complete commitment to Christ prevented him from giving his sworn allegiance to an institution not specifically Christian. In the years before 1833, there had been a growing difference of opinion among the members of the church over the application of this principle. Most felt that a Covenanter could not swear allegiance to the Constitution of the United States for two basic reasons. First, its silence on the matter of slavery gave tacit sanction to this obviously non-Christian institution. Second was the absence of the formal recognition of the sovereignty of Jesus over the nation or public acknowledgement of the authority of the law of God. These two areas had been included in the original charters of the colonies, but were absent from the U. S. Constitution.

During the War of 1812, under the pressure of showing loyalty, the Covenanter synod passed a declaration approving of the form of civil government in the land, and giving preference to it over any other government by disclaiming all allegiance to any foreign jurisdiction whatsoever. In the eyes of many, this declaration constituted a change in the accepted political sentiments of the Covenanters. In addition, one of the leading ministers in the church had openly taken the oath to the Constitution, had been naturalized as a citizen and had actually voted in an election.

Because of the apparent change, a layman in Illinois, wondering if this 1812 declaration had changed the church's stance in civil affairs, wrote in 1821 to the Synod, asking if it was OK to sit on juries. The reply of the synod was worded to the effect that nothing is prohibited except that which is truly involving immorality. In effect, the Synod took the stand that the declaration of 1812 did in fact now render involvement with the government of the United States as being *not* immoral, and changed the official position of the church. Many dissented from this change.

The matter reached the church courts when a committee appointed to draft a pastoral address to the congregations in the church included the doctrine that political dissent be left to the individual conscience. After sharp debate, the address was ordered printed without the offending paragraphs. The committee published the original draft anyway!

This resulted in a special meeting being called by those dissenting to the new position. This meeting suspended six ministers who held the new position, including the author of the 1812 declaration. At the following General Synod in 1822 there was a severe altercation and a split developed—with a minority of the ministers and about half of the congregations (holding to the new position) remaining with the General Synod, from then on referred to as "New Light" and the remainder going to what is to this day referred to as "Old Light," or officially as the Reformed Presbyterian Church, Covenanter Synod. This group continues to function as a denomination yet today. We will pick up the history of the General Synod in a later chapter.

Early in the 19th Century, it became apparent to those in the "mainline denomination that there was a need for a formal Presbyterian seminary which would be able to train clergy for the Middle States area. The Board of Trustees decided to start one at Princeton.

There should be no doubt in anyone's mind that the formation of Princeton Seminary was the most important result of the Second Awakening. Princeton Seminary would influence conservative, Bible-believing Christians in America—and not just Presbyterians—for 125 years. It's resulting Princeton Theology still remains at the very center of the heritage of the Presbyterian Church in America today.

The man who was clearly raised up by God for the purpose of founding this seminary was named Archibald Alexander. He was the third generation of Scots-Irish immigrants who grew up in the Shenandoah Valley of Virginia. He was tutored for the ministry by a pastor in Lexington, Virginia named William Graham. Soon after (in 1796), he became President of a small Presbyterian college outside of Farmville, Virginia named Hampden-Sydney. Alexander became so well known in that role that he was ultimately called to the pastorate of an influential church in Philadelphia, and we will see later in this study his strong influence lasting there until well into the 20th Century.

Alexander became a leader on the national level in the call for the formation of a Seminary. In 1812, he was rewarded by being named the first professor of the Theological Faculty at the College of New Jersey (which we now know as Princeton). For many years Alexander served by himself in this role, but it was his wisdom in developing the initial curriculum that was of utmost importance.

At the time he began, there were several prevailing theological strains in America. One was the New England Puritan tradition following Jonathan Edwards. Another was known as the New Divinity—Puritan based but more pointedly evangelical. Yet a third was the Scottish philosophical form brought with him by Witherspoon. Rather than choosing one of these three theological strains, Alexander made a different choice. While we cannot be certain of its source, it is probable that he was tutored in this somewhat different strain of theology by Graham in Lexington. Alexander's choice was to follow the Swiss Reformation theology, especially as found in the writings of Francois Turretin.

Turretin emphasized the sovereignty of God, especially in the doctrine of predestination and was a staunch defender of the authority of Scripture alone. Additionally, Turretin was the first to write a systematic theology that emphasized the overriding importance of the covenant of grace in the understanding of the Bible. These would become essential elements of the Princeton Theology of the future.

In addition to these theological emphases, Alexander brought to his position a very conservative, very non-volatile temperament. This steadiness would also become the temperament of Princeton Theology and many believe was even more important to the ability of Princeton to ward off the challenges of liberalism that would arrive later in the century from Europe.

Princeton Seminary became famous on the world stage during the reign of Alexander's successor as Principal of Princeton (as the head of the faculty was called in those days.) Charles Hodge entered the College of New Jersey in 1812 and then went immediately to study at the new seminary. In 1822, he was appointed as a Professor of Biblical Literature and from 1826 to 1828 traveled and studied extensively in Europe.

He was familiar with the more liberal theology that would find its way to the American shore.

During Hodge's fifty years on the faculty at Princeton, he helped train more than 3,000 men for the ministry—resulting in a stronger influence on religion in America in the 19th Century than any other single person. Hodge was known for his defense of and emphasis on the doctrine of biblical inerrancy. As was his mentor's personality (Alexander), Hodge's temperament was conservative and moderate in all things.

Hodge was also a great churchman and served as moderator of the Presbyterian General Assembly during the volatile years leading up to the War Between the States. He and James H. Thornwell were known as the leaders of the major factions in the church that differed on a number of crucial issues (which we will look at later in the chapter on the Southern Presbyterian Church).

As was evident in its ability to withstand the liberal theology that came to the U. S. during the last half of the 19th Century, Hodge's hallmark—as well as his most famous quote—was "A new idea never originated in this seminary!'

Hodge was followed at Princeton by Benjamin B. Warfield. He was far less colorful than his predecessor, and was not recognized as a great systematic theologian, although he wrote extensively. Notice what Francis Patton, the first official president of Princeton, had to say in the memorial address he delivered (an address intended as praise for Warfield) at First Presbyterian Church of Princeton, May 2, 1921:

Dr. Warfield was a most imposing figure. Tall, erect, with finely molded features and singular grace and courtesy of demeanor, he bore the marks of a gentleman to his fingertips. There was something remarkable about his voice. It had the liquid softness of the South rather than the metallic resonance which we look for in those who breathe the crisp air of a northern climate. His public utterance took the form of a conversational tone, and his sentences often closed with the suggestion of a rising inflection, as if he invited a hospitable reception from his hearers. He lacked the clarion tones of impassioned oratory, but oratory of this kind was not natural to him. He kept the calm level of deliberate speech, and his words proceeded out of his mouth as if they walked on velvet. But public speaking was not his chosen form of self-expression. He was pre-eminently a scholar and lived among his books. With the activities of the Church he had comparatively little to do. He seldom preached in our neighboring cities, was not prominent in debates of the General Assembly, was not a member of any of the Boards of our Church, did not serve on committees, and wasted no energy in the pleasant but perhaps unprofitable pastime of after-dinner speaking. As was to be expected, therefore, he was too much of a recluse to be what is known as a popular man.

These were comments intended to praise Warfield. We should understand, however, that Warfield's wife was very sick for many years. That kept him from traveling and limited his church involvement. Some believe his lack of great stature within the church resulted in the decline of Princeton theology and, ultimately, the fall of Princeton Seminary from leadership in the evangelical world.

We will pick up in the next chapter with the history of the third group of Presbyterians who came out of the Second Awakening on the western frontier, and examine the growth of revivalism in America.

## Chapter Eleven
## The Birth of Modern Revivalism

I n this chapter we jump back to the late 18th Century and examine the third group of Presbyterians that came out of the Second Awakening—those on the western frontier. Kentucky and Tennessee received recognition as states in 1792 and 1796, respectively although they were both sparsely populated. The largest populated city in the region was in Lexington, Kentucky with close to 2,000 people by 1800. Others such as Louisville, Frankfort, Nashville and Knoxville all supported less than 500 people.

As one would expect, the early frontier was no different than that which developed in the better known wild west. The life style was both rugged and without regard to the law. City folks were usually quite shocked by the behavior. But that did not stop Christians who had a zeal for evangelism from traveling to the frontier to share the gospel.

As strange as this may seem to folks today, the Presbyterians were as involved as anyone in the early stages of this frontier ministry. Many of the farmers in the area were from the vast number of immigrants of Scots-Irish descent and many of them had memorized the Shorter Catechism as children. So it was not uncommon to find Presbyterian ministers and evangelists among them—although most of these men came on their own without formal commissioning by a Presbytery or congregation.

The first church organized in this frontier was a Presbyterian church in Danville, Kentucky sometime around 1785. By the early 1800s, there were two presbyteries organized along the Ohio River, fed mostly by the money and people available from the large, well-to-do Presbyterian churches in the Pittsburgh area.

Two Presbyterian ministers decided to move away from the traditional, town-centered, building-facilitated ministry and take to the fields right after the turn of the century. The first was James McGready. Working closely with him was a protégé, Barton Stone. McGready ministered at the Gasper River Church and Stone had a two-congregation charge at Cane Ridge and Concord. All of these locations were within a day's buggy ride or so from Lexington, Kentucky.

The first meetings at Gasper River were mildly successful and others were immediately planned. They were called Communion services, since the rural Christians did not regularly have an opportunity to receive the Sacraments. In August of 1801, Stone organized a service in the Cane Ridge area that has become infamous. In fact, Paul Conkin, an Emeritus Distinguished Professor of History at Vanderbilt wrote an entire book about it, entitled *Cane Ridge: America's Pentecost*.

The Cane Ridge meetings lasted nearly a week. They would have gone longer, except for running out of food and water and for overtaxing what little sanitary facilities were available. At its peak there were as many as 10,000 (some say 20,000 but that's probably an exaggeration) people involved.

Even those involved in the event do not agree in their written records on what really happened. Some there were merely psychological phenomena of the time. Others say there were miracles. Stone himself records the event in his record, *A Short History of the Life of Baton W. Stone Written by Himself in Voices from Cane Ridge*, ed. Rhodes Thompson, facsimile ed. (Saint Louis, Bethany Press, 1954). He says:

Many things transpired there, which were so much like miracles, that if they were not, they had the same effects as miracles on infidels and unbelievers; for many of them by these were convinced that Jesus was the Christ, and bowed in submission to him.

One must try to imagine the setting for the event. Picture milling crowds of hardened frontier farmers—tobacco-chewing, tough spoken, profane, famous for alcoholic thirsts. They would have bawdy acting wives and great broods of undisciplined children. There would be a rough clearing of the land with rows of wagons and crude tents. Evangelists would speak from hastily constructed wooden platforms, or simply climb up into a tree. By night, there would be campfires glowing—making eerie shadows. (And remember, most farmers had never been awake all night before.) This would have been the most significant social occasion in the life of these farmers—who were by their very nature very lonely people.

With that picture in mind, here is a description of some of what happened during the Cane Ridge Revival as people reacted to the preaching of the gospel—again from the *Short Life of Stone*:

The bodily agitations or exercises, attending the excitement in the beginning of this century, were various, and called by various names.

...The falling exercise was very common among all classes, the saints and sinners of every age and of every grade, from the philosopher to the clown. The subject of this exercise would, generally, with a piercing scream, fall like a log on the floor, earth, or mud, and appear as dead...

129

The jerks cannot be so easily described. Sometimes the subject of the jerks would be affected in some one member of the body, and sometimes the whole system. When the head alone was affected, it would be jerked backward and forward, or from side to side...When the whole system was affected, I have seen the person stand in one place, and jerk backward and forward in quick succession, and their head nearly touching the floor behind and before...

The dancing exercise. This generally began with the jerks, and was peculiar to the professors of religion. The subject, after jerking awhile, began to dance, and then the jerks would cease. Such dancing was indeed heavenly to the spectators; there was nothing in it like levity, nor calculated to excite levity in the beholders.

The barking exercise, (as opposers contemptuously called it,) was nothing but the jerks. A person affected with the jerks, especially in his head, would often make a grunt, or bark, if you please, from the suddenness of the jerk...

The laughing exercise was frequent, confined solely with the religious. It was a loud, hearty laughter...it excited laughter in none else. The subject appeared rapturously solemn, and his laughter excited solemnity in saints and sinners.

I shall close this chapter with the singing exercise. This is more unaccountable than any thing else I ever saw. The subject in a very a happy state of mind would sing most melodiously, not from the mouth or nose, but entirely in the breast, the sounds issuing from thence. Such music silenced every thing, and attracted the attention of all. It was most heavenly.

Once word of Cane Ridge got out, it led to a widespread phenomenon of more camp meetings and revivals. In a very few years, however, the churches in the region grew in number but not in quality of members.

We must also understand that both the Methodists and Baptists were very active in the region and conducted similar types of meetings and revivals. At the end of the day, they were much more successful in terms of numbers of people who affiliated with them than were the Presbyterians, who felt such man-man methods were not properly biblical.

Presbyterians have always been committed to particular church forms and practices. One of the core values of Presbyterians is the education and instruction of both children and adults in Christian principles. They had a rich but set doctrinal system that wasn't easy to simplify for the frontier, and they always required a well-educated ministry. Not many ministers were available for the rapid growth that was occurring in the frontier.

Soon a group of six Presbyterian ministers—among them Barton Stone himself—separated and organized their own presbytery—called the Springfield (Illinois) Presbytery. They became critical not only of Reformed theology but also of church government. They quickly decided they were Congregationalists and stopped calling themselves Presbyterians. In 1804, they took on the simple name of the Christian Church. Two of these six went on to become founders of the Shaker movement. Two others ultimately returned to the mainline church. But Barton Stone and one other remained.

Parallel to this, a Presbyterian minister named Thomas Campbell, a pastor in Western Pennsylvania, was disciplined by his presbytery for being too lax in admitting people to the

Lord's Supper. In 1807, he withdrew to independence and began his own ministry, called Christian Association of Washington (PA). Thomas never intended to form a new denomination, but his son, Alexander was more controversial. Alexander Campbell took control of the movement in 1813. He had trained for the ministry in Scotland, but had non-Presbyterian leanings even then. He put an emphasis only on New Testament Christianity and sought to develop a "primitive" or "restored" church form.

Several years later, Campbell's group merged with a group known as Christian Baptist. In 1827, another young schoolteacher with roots in Scotland (who had been influenced by another Christian Baptist teaching in Steubenville, Ohio) began to formally advocate a denomination based on these primitive church principals. So the Campbellites and other Christian Baptists joined to form the denomination known today as the Disciples of Christ.

In 1813, a larger group broke away from the mainline Presbyterians in Kentucky and Tennessee and formed a new denomination named for a nearby river—Cumberland Presbyterian Church. They adopted a revised version (with Arminian theology) of the Westminster standards. It is worth noting that a large group of the Cumberlands re-merged with the mainline Presbyterians in the early 1900s. The remaining Cumberlands today are firmly Arminian and also deeply affect by theological liberalism.

Clearly, the desire of a form of revival brought about by the methods and work of man apart from the leading of God's spirit was beginning to rule the day. As the nation expanded into what was then known at the Old Northwest (upstate New York, Western Pennsylvania, Ohio, Indiana and Illinois), there was also great church expansion as well. The

Congregationalists and Presbyterians formed a Plan of Union in 1801 to deal with this expansion together. The plan stated that after a new church was started, the congregation could decide to which denomination it wanted to belong.

The New England theology of the Congregationalists (by now known as the New Haven Theology) began to water down the teaching and beliefs of many Presbyterian ministers and churches. Lyman Beecher, a well-known Presbyterian pastor in Boston, became President of Lane Seminary in Cincinnati. He was taken to trial by his presbytery in 1835 for theological error. While he was not convicted, one can begin to see the problems growing in Presbyterian churches.

Entering this situation was one Charles Grandison Finney. Finney was born in 1792 in Connecticut. At the age of two, his family moved to upstate New York. Finney studied law and began to practice in the town of Adams, New York. There he came under the influence of a young Presbyterian minister. He liked this young minister very much on a personal basis, but as he studied, he decided he disliked Presbyterian theology.

One day while reading his Bible, he had what he described as a dramatic conversion experience, which he said brought him to "a retainer from the Lord Jesus Christ to plead his cause." So, he immediately began preaching. Even though he had no theological or practical training at all, he became famous in the region. Almost out of necessity due to his popularity with the people, the St. Lawrence Presbytery reluctantly licensed him to preach.

Finney began to conduct great revivals throughout the region in Western New York. (This region would later become known as the "burned over" region because of so many different forms of teaching finding roots here—such as

Mormons, dispensationalists, several famous mediums, and even P. T. Barnum.)

Finney developed and began to teach what he called a New Measures style of evangelism. He said it was OK to use the language of street people rather than "King James English." He promoted the value of long series of meetings in one place—always for at least a week—and thus he would preach almost every single night of the year. He also developed the use of an "anxious bench" in which he would encourage those who felt they were "almost saved" to sit up front.

Finney was the first evangelist to regularly use individual public testimonies of conversion experience as part of his meetings—and even would allow women to speak to the crowds of people in this way. He was the first to use mass publicity as a means to gather people to attend his revivals—including the distribution of flyers describing the place, date and time of each meeting.

Finally, Finney simply renounced the Presbyterian Church and went out on his own, declaring himself to be an independent Congregational minister. He became ill from overwork and had to give up revival preaching. Thus he moved to Oberlin, Ohio to become a Professor of Theology and ultimately President of Oberlin College.

Finney taught a theological position that was clearly different from traditional, conservative Reformed Theology as originally held by the Puritans and early Congregationalists and that still held by the Presbyterians. He put a human emphasis on the process of conversion, rather than seeing God as the center of the source. Finney taught that man is able to save himself; that sin is voluntary and therefore completely avoidable. He even taught that complete holiness (perfection) is possible in this life.

While the offering of invitations may have been invented in the fields of Kentucky, Finney is clearly responsible for making the invitation system the heart and soul of Modern Revivalism. Finney said, "Revival is not a miracle, or dependent on a miracle in any sense. It is a purely philosophical, scientific result of the right use of constituted means." With Charles Finney, the "invitation system" was born. It may well have resulted in those denominations and faith groups outside the Reformed community having the larger number of members on their rolls at the beginning of the 21$^{st}$ Century.

It is worth taking some time at this point to discuss the theological implications of this invitation system developed by Finney and others. It has become an essential part of religious practice in many different churches, most of whom find their roots in this 19$^{th}$ Century Revivalism that we've been discussing, and the daughter of Revivalism known as Pentecostalism. And of course, the repute and achievement of Billy Graham are built upon his use of the invitation system. It also affected many of the more conservative Presbyterian congregations, especially in the South.

Those—like Graham and others who use the invitation system generally give three reasons for its use. The first is that Jesus always called people publicly and this can be seen in his frequently used words such as *"Follow me"* or *"Whoever shall confess me before men, I will confess before my father in heaven."* Second is the psychological argument which says that the very act of "coming out" makes a decision settled in an individual's mind. Once other people have seen you make a statement by raising your hand or walking forward, it is much, much harder to change your mind—your friends and family will

135

not think well of you if you do that! Third, the invitation has value as a visual demonstration to others yet uncommitted. When the typical moral and reputable person hears an invitation, he will normally think at first, "That's for some religious zealot, not for me." But then when he sees dozens, hundreds, or even thousands of other typical moral and reputable persons walking forward to respond to an invitation, he'll begin to consider the invitation for himself.

But are these three arguments biblically sound? Surely if they are so normatively practiced, they must be biblical, right? In fact, when I was first ordained and took a pastorate in Savannah, Georgia I heard that some of the elders in a sister church just a couple of dozen blocks away from my congregation were saying (behind my back, of course) that I was a liberal—I wasn't biblical enough—because I would not practice the invitation system. That has become a litmus test in the eyes of many "conservative" Christians.

We don't have time in this brief work to answer this question thoroughly. I would recommend that you obtain a copy of a 38-page pamphlet entitled *The Invitation System* by Iain Murray, a well known British minister and author (especially in the area of the Puritans and biographies of great evangelical leaders). (Carlisle, PA: Banner of Truth, 1967). What follows is a summary of Murray's work.

Certainly, we cannot take the words of Jesus to Matthew in Matthew 9:9, *"Follow me,"* spoken literally 2,000 years ago, as a call to take a specific action today. We can't literally "come to Jesus"—he is located in Heaven. While we can follow him in term of following his teachings and his example, this certainly is not any sort of actual following in terms of physical action. So on the face, this cannot be used as proof for an invitation system.

Another common verse used to support an invitation system is Matthew 10:32, which reads: *"So everyone who acknowledges me before men, I also will acknowledge before my Father who is in heaven...:* Does this require an immediate action such as walking forward at a meeting to fulfill? A credible confession of our faith is of course necessary when we are asked about our relationship to Jesus—but these are words, not actions. These are followed by a demonstration in our life style of what we believe—not by taking a few steps to the front of a stadium or church building. Besides, the words we say and the life-style we live themselves are not the source of our salvation anyway. They are simply Spirit-given proofs of the conversion that has previously taken place.

Some have argued that the use of the invitation system is optional, that conversion can take place with or without the use of the system. While that may be true, it certainly is, in and of itself, evidence that the system is not the one taught in the Bible, or else it would not be an option.

Turning now to the second argument—the psychological issue that says "there is something about coming forward that settles it." Evangelists who use the invitation system will say something like, "Once a person has been made aware of his troubled condition of failing to have the promise of heaven and, in fact, learning his destiny is eternal separation from God in hell, then the right emotional outlet must be provided."

There may be a glimmer of truth in this argument from a psychological view, just as the emotional "working up" of a crowd in some different venue might produce desired results. At the time of this writing, a series of Live-Aid concerts are being conducted on a world-wide basis—seeking the forgiving of Third World debt by government and banks controlled by wealthy societies and people. Even if time produces such a result (which many doubt will be the case), it is not in and of itself evidence that those involved in Christian evangelism must use the method.

The real issue here is this—is some psychological induced event necessary for someone to become a Christian? What do we say of those millions of people who have never had such a psychological experience? Are we to believe they are not converted? Of course not. And is it possible for someone to experience some psychological event, brought on by the right set of circumstances—of hearing the right words, of being asked to respond at the correct time, walking forward to make a profession of faith—and that person turn out to never be a Christian? Of course it is! The world is filled with people who once walked an aisle but are now and have for many years been living a life that shows no evidence of conversion, no fruit of the presence of the Holy Spirit in their life. So the psychological argument of necessity is not valid as a proof for use of the invitation system.

How about the effects of seeing many others make a decision as a way to influence an individual? This is one of the main reasons the Billy Graham Crusades have insisted on using the system. Graham knows full well that many who walk the aisle are never converted. But yet, he believes that the very seeing of many come forward—either in person or on TV—has some value in affecting the decisions of some individuals. But that would mean that each individual makes his or her own decision to become a Christian. Is that what the Bible teaches? Well, not if you understand the Scriptures within the framework we have been calling the Reformed faith, that which is at the heart of Presbyterian churches.

In order to hold to the teaching known as Decisional Regeneration, there is clear demonstration of the Arminian position that one has the ability to be involved in his or her own salvation. It denies Total Depravity, which teaches us that our wills are so affected by sin we are unable to take any action of our own that saves us. It denies Unconditional Election, which teaches that God, before the foundations of the world, makes the determination of who will be saved and does not have to wait to see what happens in history.

All of this is not to say that one should never make a public invitation for people to profess Christ. While spending three days at home sick while my wife was attending a series of evangelistic services at a Reformed Presbyterian Church in New Jersey, I became a Christian simply by reading the Gospel of John over and over again. The Spirit worked, as he always does, through the ordinary means of grace—in this case, the word of God coupled with years of prayer on the part of my wife and my mother-in-law.

The fourth night I was well and, not having mentioned anything to my wife, told her I wanted to go to the final service. It was a Monday night and in the eyes of everyone else, the evangelistic meeting was over. The preacher, a Seminary professor who used the message to preach on the need for an educated clergy as a way to help the church continue to support their denominational seminary, was moved by the Spirit to make an invitation after the sermon.

He had not presented the gospel during the sermon. He had not used an invitation during the previous evangelistic messages, he was convinced of the problems with the invitation system. But that night, he asked for a show of hands of anyone who wanted to make a profession of faith in Jesus. My hand went up. I was ready to make a profession of faith, but I had already become a Christian over the weekend, by reading the Bible.

So, there is nothing inherently wrong with an occasional invitation. But a "system"—*à la* Charles Finney—that says that anyone not using the invitation system is not doing biblical evangelism…is just not correct. Only God knows which denomination and faith groups have the largest percentage of committed Bible-believing Christians, who are making an impact within God's kingdom on earth.

## Chapter Twelve
## The Battle for the Bible – Christianity and Liberalism

Before we try to understand any further Presbyterian history in America, it is necessary to take some time to understand the origins and basic principles involved in the rise of what is called Liberalism.

Christianity is based on an account of something that happened historically in time and space in the 1st Century. Before the validity and true meaning of that event can be received, however, certain presuppositions must be accepted. The Christian gospel consists of an account of how God saved man, so there are two great presuppositions.

The first great presupposition involves the doctrine of God. We must begin with the presupposition that God exists; that there is indeed a living and true God. As Francis Schaeffer (certainly one of the greatest thinkers, disciplers and evangelists of the later decades of the 20th Century—and very importantly, a Presbyterian minister) puts it, "he is there."

A secondary part of this first presupposition involves understanding not only that God is there, but also that "he is not silent." (By the way, one of Schaeffer's most important books goes by the title, *He is There and He Is Not Silent* (Carol Stream, IL: Tyndale, 1972). The concept that God is not silent is just another way of saying that God has spoken, that he has revealed himself. And, as essentially all Bible-believing Christians understand, God reveals himself in two ways: General Revelation and Special Revelation.

General Revelation refers to the fact that we can understand that God exists without ever knowing there is such a thing as the Bible. We know God exists just by looking at the creation—the galaxies, the complexity of man, the very existence of life. But, as we will quickly see, it is on the presupposition that God has spoken in Special Revelation and that this Special Revelation (which is to say, the Bible) is without error that the battleground that was initially drawn between Christianity and Liberalism and over which there is still an ongoing war. To understand the Presbyterian Church in America today, you must understand the battles over biblical inerrancy.

The second great presupposition involves the doctrine of Man. This presupposition also has two parts. The first part is to understand that man is made in the image of God. He is a special creature (as opposed to the teaching of evolution.) If one cannot agree that human beings are special creatures, one's understanding of the Bible and the Christian faith will always be faulty. In fact, the PCA has twice made judicial decisions that state clearly that anyone who believes in evolution—even including that which is known as "theistic evolution" (which is to say that evolution exists but it is overseen by God) not only cannot hold office in the PCA, but may not even teach within the Church.

The second part of this understanding of the doctrine of Man is in the area of sin. We must understand that man, because of the fall of Adam and Even in the Garden of Eden, is polluted with original sin, and as such, is unable to save himself. This is why the doctrine of Total Depravity has been defended so vigorously over the centuries: the Synod of Dordt, the Westminster Assembly, Whitefield versus the Wesleys;

Princeton Theology versus Revivalism. If you do not accept this presupposition, you end up with a man who is somehow and someway basically good and therefore is able to save himself—or at a minimum is able to cooperate in his salvation. If that were the case, there would be no need for the miraculous intervention of God.

A true understanding of the biblical plan of salvation requires that we make these two presuppositions: God is there and he is not silent; coupled with the understanding that man is created in the image of God, but is a sinner and is unable to save himself.

For purpose of this chapter, I will be using the terms "Liberalism" and "liberal" in a very narrow, technical way—and probably in the only way they should be used when one discusses religion. Liberalism is a set of ideas and doctrine that grew out of German theology in the 19th Century (more a little later on the history). Liberalism attacks the two basic presuppositions of Christianity head on.

Liberalism says that God does not exist—at least not as a living person. To a theological liberal, God is an idea, something that is wholly other than a person. Since God is not a living person, he does not exist in "personality"—he is not, objectively speaking, "there." Since ideas exist only in the minds of human beings, and since God is only an idea, he is not "there."

Since God is not there, it logically follows that he has not spoken; he has not revealed himself. He has not set forth his word in Scripture. Since there is no divine truth to the Bible— since it is simply a compilation of man's ideas about what God might be like—then there is no necessity to believe the contents of the Bible. Therefore, many of the Old Testament narratives are just myth. And, in the New Testament, while there may or may not have been a historical person called Jesus, he certainly was not God and he did not perform miracles.

Since there is no God and since he has not spoken, we are left only with man and his ideas about God. Man, according to liberals, is basically a good creature, he merely learns bad things. In the words of West Side Story, he's depraved because he's deprived.

The real harm of evolution lies in the understanding of liberals who believe that man is constantly improving, getting better, and therefore is able to save himself. He has no need for God. This results in a type of small-"h" humanism, a focus on man and his ability rather than on God. To a liberal, humanism focuses on what religious thoughts and ideas can do for man. The source of these thoughts, of this kind of religion, derives from man's own reason and experience.

Humanism is not new. It was inherent in the thought and writings of the Greeks. It was very active in the medieval church. It was rejected by the Reformation, although it continued in Roman Catholic circles. And it really grew up into full bloom and focus in the 19th Century with the advancement of philosophical movement known as the Enlightenment and the knowledge of science. We find this humanism in various forms.

Subjective Romanticism is the thought and writing of a philosopher named Rousseau, which flourished in the early 19<sup>th</sup> Century. It was a reaction against the Enlightenment. Rousseau objected to the coldness and pure logic of science, and emphasized human experience as the source of knowledge.

Charles Darwin's Theory of Evolution is another type of humanism. In his famous book *Origin of the Species*, which he published in 1859, Darwin was seeking a new way to affirm the relativity of all truth. He wanted to show that nothing is absolute, that everything in creation is in flux: it is now, and always has been, developing. Darwin wasn't as much a scientist as he was a philosopher.

Coming out of this same cauldron of humanism is 19<sup>th</sup> Century Socialism. Especially in the writings of Karl Marx, you see the emphasis on man and a stress on human economics, totally denying even the hint of religion. In looking at his life story, you find that Marx was affected deeply by the way his Jewish father was treated very badly by some Christians, and he grew to hate Christianity and the church. He turned to human experience as the solution to all of man's problems.

In addition to humanism taking hold of philosophy, science and economics, it also took hold of theological study and writings in the theory that has come to be known as Higher Criticism. To understand Higher Criticism, we have got to understand Friedrich Schliermacher, the Father of Modern Theology.

Schliermacher was born in Germany in 1768. He grew up in a Moravian home with strong pietistic teachings and experiences. He went to a school run by Moravians and learned not only their Bible stories and theology, but also participated in their religious practices, which stressed feelings and experience. When he went to college, Friedrich intended to become a Lutheran clergyman, but first wanted to study philosophy. Thus he became an avid student of Immanuel Kant.

Kant taught that all religious knowledge comes from within a human being; that God was merely a set of ideas and those ideas formed feelings and emotions inside of people that worked themselves out in religion. Schliermacher tried to put the philosophy of Kant together with the theology he had learned growing up, and was currently studying in graduate school. Kant concluded that the essence of theology is a "feeling of absolute dependence." If we felt dependent on God, then that would cause God to exist and we would be in a theological relationship with him.

When he finished his training, Schliermacher was ordained as a minister and was assigned to work as a hospital chaplain. He worked and lived in Berlin, and came into contact with many people in the medical field. Through them, he met many other intellectuals. He was unique as a clergyman—working and traveling in scientific, intellectual and literary circles at the same time.

Schliermacher taught that one must be *both* a theologian and a modern man. You did not have to sacrifice one for the other as people had been doing for centuries. Modern man had insisted that theology was useless. Theologians had insisted that science was demonic at worst and irrelevant at best. Schliermacher wanted to bring the two disciplines together—a noble goal, to be sure, but accomplished in a non-biblical way.

He emphasized that what is important about theology is not whether it is true or not, but what it means for the individual. It is not necessary to believe and accept all of the Bible, but rather to try to see what the history and description of religion in the Bible meant to each individual person. From this teaching developed a school of thought known as Higher Criticism, in which people assumed that the Bible was made up of differing manmade stories and real scholars had to sort the stories out according to the various human sources.

A famous example of this is the JEDP theory of the authorship of the Pentateuch—the first five books of the Old Testament. Higher Criticism teaches that there are four different authors of these five books (rather than one author, Moses, as Bible-believing Christians teach). You can distinguish these four authors by their styles. One author always used Jehovah for God's name; he's the "J." Another always used "Elohim" for God's name; he's the "E." The third wrote Deuteronomy; he's the "D." And the fourth was a priest who wrote much of Leviticus, the priestly codes; he, of course, is the "P."

According to followers of Higher Criticism, Jesus was simply the one man in history in whom the consciousness of God reached its perfection. Man today would be redeemed by the same dynamic that operated in Jesus, so we should try to imitate Jesus and develop a deeper consciousness of God ourselves. The more we felt religious, the better we would be. What Christians called the Holy Spirit, Schliermacher said was simply the consciousness of God in Jesus operating in the church.

Schliermacher actually hoped and believed that the whole world would be transformed through the church. His main work, entitled *Christian Faith* was published in 1821. In this book, he took centuries-old theological and biblical concepts and terms and filled them with different meanings. Commenting once on Charles Hodge (the outspoken evangelical theological of the day), Schliermacher inferred that Hodge was saved because he felt saved, that there was no objective reality to salvation; it was simply the height of religious feelings. (This is the way he understood his pietistic, Moravian roots—and it shows us today the danger of "feeling-based" religious practice.)

Ultimately, Schliermacher deserted God's revelation in the Bible all together and replaced it with humanistic religion, with man at the center. This is the essence of theological Liberalism. All current modernism flows from Schliermacher.

So, what has happened to Liberalism in the theological world? Everyone seeks to answer the wrong question. Rather than asking the essential biblical question, "How may I know the living and true God and his only Son, Jesus?" they ask instead, "What is there to prevent discovery of a higher form than Christ?" If religion is simply a set of religious feelings, and if Christians think that the ultimate set of feelings were those that Jesus had, why not look for something even better? The late 19th Century saw more and more radical forms of Higher Criticism and Liberalism. People were sure that man could solve all the problems of the universe.

Then came the Great War—the one we call World War I. With this immense demonstration of man's inhumanity, the idea that secular thought and science would save the world quickly was dashed, and along with it many of the theological positions of Liberalism. There was a movement of people that wanted to return to more traditional Christianity. This movement became know as Neo-Orthodoxy, a so-called "new" orthodox theology.

The problem with Neo-Orthodoxy, whose primary spokesman in the 20th Century was Karl Barth (more on him later), is that it was a reaction only against Schliermacher and Liberalism. It still retained much of the teaching of Higher Criticism which said that the Bible was not the inerrant word of God.

Ultimately, without the concepts of the infallibility and inerrancy of the Bible, there is no defense against any form of Liberalism or Modernism—not even Neo-Orthodoxy. This is why Charles Hodge and the Princeton theology were so important in 19th Century America. The 3,000 ministers that Hodge produced fought to keep this kind of Liberalism away from America for the most part.

But there were still a growing number of people in America who continued to study and believe the basics of Liberalism. One was Albert Schweitzer. Known today for his great medical work, Schweitzer was only secondarily a medical doctor. He was primarily a Liberal theologian. In 1907, Schweitzer published a doctoral dissertation in theology from which his popular book, *The Quest for the Historical Jesus,* was drawn.

He went to Africa as a medical missionary with the primary purpose of proving his Liberal theology. In Schweitzer's view, it was important to separate the historical Jesus from the rest of religious feelings. Some Liberals had taught that Jesus never even existed. Schweitzer sought to prove that in fact he did exist as a historical character, but that his existence was not crucial for faith. He claimed one could "believe" with or without a historical Jesus.

Another key individual in American Liberal theological circles was Karl Barth. Swiss Reformed in background, Barth taught that "god" was a transcendent being (not a person, as Christians understand, but also not just a set of ideas either). And this transcendent being confronted man through his "Word." Primarily, to Barth, the Bible does not contain propositional truth—it contains information about Jesus, who himself is God's "Word." Barth says that each person approaches the Bible differently, and it depends entirely on what that person feels as to what is gained from the Bible, and how it affects a person's life.

Let's try to sum this up a little bit. Christianity is based on an account of something that happened in space and time in the First Century. But before that account can be received and understood and believed, certain presuppositions must be accepted. The Christian gospel is an account of how God saved man, so the two great presuppositions are God (a living God) and Man (a sinful man).

The liberal doctrine of God and the liberal doctrine of Man are both diametrically opposed to the Christian view.

What is more, this affects everything—the very message of the Bible, our attitude toward Jesus, and the source of salvation. How does this liberal doctrine get into the church? Essentially, these views get into the church when the leadership (in the case of Presbyterians, the elders) accepts into membership of the church men and women who do not give a credible profession of faith. Individuals who do not take the classic church membership vows that are based on those two great presuppositions.

In case you may not have taken those vows yourself, or more likely, have forgotten them, let me repeat them for you here—they are the first two of a total of five that members of PCA churches take:

1. Do you acknowledge yourselves to be sinners in the sight of God, justly deserving his displeasure, and without hope save in his sovereign mercy?

2. Do you believe in the Lord Jesus Christ as the Son of God, and Savior of sinners, and do you receive and rest upon him alone for salvation as he is offered in the gospel?

If people enter the church, who do not believe the teachings of the Bible underlying those vows, they will not care if they hear preaching or are taught lessons that are opposed to the Christian views. They will send representatives to presbytery and General Assembly who do not care if the decisions of those bodies are biblical, especially the decisions of a presbytery to license and ordain men to preach the gospel who do not hold those essential Christian views. Liberalism always starts with church leaders who no longer care about basic biblical theological beliefs.

As we'll see in the next two chapters, first Liberalism took hold of the Northern Presbyterian Church and brought about the theological downfall of Princeton Seminary in the 1920s. Several decades later, the Neo-Orthodoxy of Barth took hold of the Southern Presbyterian Church and came into the Christian education material known as the Covenant Life curriculum that allowed Liberalism into that denomination.

## Chapter Thirteen
## Theological Decline in the Northern Presbyterian Church

Most people think that the mainline Presbyterian Church split in the 19th Century over the issue of slavery. That was never the major issue. More than two decades prior to the North-South division of the Church, the mainline church began the first in a series of many splits, that will become almost normative for many decades as well see in the next chapter, entitled "The Split P's."

You will recall we mentioned in Chapter Eleven that, in an effort to advance the establishment of churches in the Old Northwest, there was a plan developed with the Congregationalists. This grew out of an even larger proposed plan. After the turn of the century, there grew in America a strong sense of cooperation among varied groups in many different arenas, including the church. This could certainly be looked on as a truly ecumenical movement. As an integral part of this movement, a sense of cooperation came about between the Congregationalists and Presbyterians, especially in the area of evangelism. Both of these groups had a more or less Reformed doctrinal stance, but varied mostly in the area of church government.

The Presbyterians suggested a Plan of Union for the two groups, which was adopted in 1801. The plan kept distinct the denominations, but a local church could be represented in the courts of both denominations at the same time. The union showed itself especially in the area of joint boards, particularly in the area of evangelism.

There was a large group within the Presbyterian Church who were dissatisfied with the Plan of Union, principally because the churches that were newly created as a result of the joint evangelism were not truly Presbyterian. It was impossible to properly carry out effective discipline. The issue of denominational control of the boards was also a point of disagreement. In addition to these matters of church government and discipline, there were also doctrinal issues which formed a base for the controversy. The group supporting the Plan of Union tended to deviate more from the strict Calvinism of the Westminster Standards, and began following the more Arminian doctrines that we saw active on the western frontier.

At the General Assembly of 1837, matters came to a head when the conservative element who were opposed to the Plan of Union found themselves in the majority at the Assembly. They voted to dissolve the Plan of Union and to dismiss from the denomination four synods what had been formed under it. This of course caused a definite division within the church. The split turned out to be just about 50-50, with the conservative (known as the Old School) group being granted by the courts the right of maintaining the status as the continuing church, while the New School became a new denomination.

As the War Between the States approached, the issue of slavery and support of the Federal government inevitably came up within the various national churches in America. The Old School Presbyterian Assembly was no exception. At its meeting in May of 1861, Dr. Gardiner Spring offered resolutions committing the church to the Federal cause, recommending a day of prayer, professing loyalty to the Federal government, and declaring it a duty to support the government and to preserve the Union.

Those who were against the Spring Resolutions (as they have forever since been known) were not against them in spirit, but were protesting against the Assembly's action upon political issues and in determining questions of civil allegiance. These men felt the purpose of the church was spiritual and that they should not meddle in political matters. During the meeting, the commissioners were continually receiving telegrams advising them how to vote. Under this great pressure of public opinion, the Spring Resolutions were adopted after five days of debate.

Consequently, some churches in the Old School in the South used the passing of these resolutions as a reason for leaving and joining with other churches in the South (which had previously pulled out of the New School Presbyterian Assembly.) The Old School churches, and thus their theological positions, were clearly in the majority. This group formed a denomination, which was commonly called the Southern Presbyterian Church. After the War Between the States, it became known as the Presbyterian Church in the United States (PCUS). The Northern church was known as the Presbyterian Church in the United States of America (PCUSA).

After the War Between the States, there again grew up a spirit of unity within the nation, especially as the West was being opened and evangelism became a large task on the frontier. Even during the War, a group at the Old School Assembly of 1862 (the part that was in the North) initiated a proposal for an exchange of commissioners with the New School. There appeared to be a development within the New School of a stronger sense of the church than they had held during the Plan of Union days, and they had begun to conduct their missionary work by denominational committees quite similar to the Old School boards.

At the same time, there appeared to be among many of the Old School less of an emphasis on doctrinal issues in the church. The total result of all this was that in 1869, the Old and New Schools reunited on the basis of the Westminster Standards—"pure and simple"—as the effecting document stated.

This merger is a most important point in the history of the PCUSA (Northern Church). It is felt by many conservative scholars that this union should never have taken place. One called it "one of the tragic events in Presbyterian history." It appears that there was a significant relaxing of doctrinal principles on the part of the Old School at the time of the merger. This fear came to fruition within two decades, and came to the forefront at Union Seminary in New York surrounding a controversy involving a Professor of Theology who was promoted to a named chair.

Union Seminary, as the name implies, was a Presbyterian-based seminary that grew out of the Plan of Union days with Congregationalists. It was formed in 1836 and the majority (not all) of its faculty had been New School men. After the merger between the Old and New Schools in 1869, there was increased Old School influence.

Charles Briggs came from an Old School background and originally held a biblical and evangelical view of the Bible, but decided to pursue doctoral studies in Germany (as many young men did in those days, believing they were far advanced over the younger American schools). In those studies, he was deeply influenced by the teachings of Higher Criticism and upon his return to the U.S. was called as a Professor at Union Seminary in 1874. (This is why it was so important to study the role of Higher Criticism as we did in the previous chapter.)

In 1890, the board of Union Seminary invited Dr. Briggs to assume a newly funded and named Chair of Biblical Theology—a high honor to a distinguished professor. But the address he gave at his inauguration dinner on January 20, 1891 acted as a fuse to light the fuel of the continuing battle for the Bible within the Northern Presbyterian Church. In his address, which was entitled "The Authority of Holy Scripture," Briggs blatantly and clearly spoke of the fact that the Bible was one of three different, independent sources of divine authority—teaching that God equally uses the Bible, the Church, and reason to reveal his will to man. He went so far as to use three illustrations of very famous British church leaders to make his point.

For the method of reason, he used the well-known Unitarian minister and professor, James Martineau, who denied the deity of Christ. For the method of the Church, he used John Henry Newman, a Roman Catholic cardinal who had passed away just a few months earlier. For the method of the Bible, he used Charles Spurgeon, the greatest preacher of the 19th Century in England (if not the world). Additionally in the speech, Briggs denied the verbal inspiration of the Scriptures, the inerrancy of the Scriptures and the existence of miracles. The gauntlet had been thrown.

Almost immediately, members of the Presbytery of New York City filed charges against Briggs, and he came to trial in a Presbytery committee meeting that October. The charges were dismissed by more than a 2-1 vote, without examination of his views, while commissioners stressed that the church should intentionally be diverse. The charges were appealed to the General Assembly who, at their 1892 meeting, overwhelmingly voted to order New York City Presbytery to take up the issues in the case. The following January, they did, acquitting Briggs of heresy. Ignoring calls of the large majority of members of the presbytery to allow diversity, the commissioners who brought the original charges again appealed to the General Assembly. The trial was held at the meeting of the General Assembly in 1893 and the vote was overwhelmingly (by almost eighty percent) to convict Briggs of heresy. They removed his ministerial credentials.

Briggs himself moved into the Episcopal Church and remained on the faculty of Union Seminary. Shortly thereafter, the Board of Trustees of Union Seminary voted to remove the seminary from the Presbyterian denomination and they have been independent ever since—currently being the theological faculty of Columbia University.

While it was a good and necessary thing to expel Briggs from the PCUSA, it appears that the conservatives within the denomination felt that through this one event they had successfully expelled all Liberalism from the church. As history was soon to reveal, this was not the case.

It was not only Presbyterians who were battling the effects of Liberalism. Every mainline denomination was going through similar battles. But the Presbyterians were the ones that had all the "big names" of the day and thus got most of the press.

In 1909, two wealthy laymen in Chicago decided to underwrite the publication of a series of books entitled *The Fundamentals* and distribute copies to every minister, Sunday school director, missionary and anyone else involved in full-time Christian work throughout the English speaking world. While 300,000 copies were initially distributed, ultimately over three million volumes were distributed worldwide.

Although a total of twelve volumes were finally published, five of the issues raised in these books quickly rose throughout the evangelical Christian world and were recognized as basic statements in opposition to the heresy that had become apparent in the Higher Criticism that had entered theological teaching. These defined the five essential issues where the battle over authority of Scripture was being waged.

These were not then nor ever the only essential doctrines in the Christian faith, but rather, they were the issues where the battle was being fought against the Liberals and the place where evangelicals could all unite. You can see the similarity to the Canons of Dordt. Remember, the five points of Dordt (frequently called the five points of Calvinism) were never the only (nor even the most important) doctrines in the Reformed faith—they were simply the point at which the attack was mounted.

These five areas were 1) the virgin birth as literal truth, 2) the fact of a substitutionary atonement, 3) the physical resurrection of Jesus from the dead, 4) the imminent physical Second Coming of Christ and 5) the absolute inerrancy of the Scriptures. The five areas quickly became known as the Fundamentals and those holding to those doctrines became known as Fundamentalists. The General Assembly of the PCUSA affirmed these five Fundamentals at their meetings of 1910 and 1916.

During this period, a Baptist minister named Harry Emerson Fosdick was called to be a professor of Practical Theology at the now independent Union Seminary in 1915. Being well known as one of the best preachers in the country, the congregation at First Presbyterian Church in New York called him to a position as an Associate Pastor and Stated Supply (a regular preacher who has not been called to be Senior Pastor. Without becoming a Presbyterian himself, Fosdick was the regular preacher at First Church, New York.

It was quite common in those days for the New York Times to include the full manuscript of a Sunday sermon in their Monday editions (which were traditionally slim because of lack of news generated over the weekend). Fosdick was frequently included as one whose sermons were transcribed and printed.

In 1922, Fosdick preached a sermon entitled "Shall The Fundamentalists Win?" Fosdick saw two groups within Protestant churches, which included the Presbyterians: those who were Fundamentalists and the other (in which he recognized his inclusion) whom he defined as the Modernists. He called for the coexistence of both groups and for the church to maintain a tolerant, inclusive attitude. (Does any of this sound familiar today?) Another way to put this theme, which we see repeated over and over again in subsequent years would be "Can't we all just get along?"

At the 1923 Assembly, there was a battle for the office of Moderator and William Jennings Bryan, former Secretary of State and a ruling elder from the conservative wing of the church lost by a handful of votes. A Moderator had great power to appoint members of standing committees. However, this Assembly, in dealing with the Fosdick issue at First Church, New York, passed a substitute motion from the floor directing the Presbytery of New York to require that the teaching of all its churches conform to the Bible and the Westminster Standards, and also affirmed for the third time the five Fundamentals of the Christian faith. While the conservative wing considered this a great victory, it was at best a short-lived one.

In fact, while not mentioned often in the press accounts of the day (but to become crystal clear later), there were elections to the boards of the church—especially to the boards of Princeton Seminary—that began to place control of the denomination clearly in the hands of the liberals. This full control was finalized by the 1925 General Assembly.

The year between the 1923 and 1924 Assemblies was filled with debate from both sides. J. Gresham Machen, a professor at Princeton Seminary wrote a small book entitled *Christianity and Liberalism* (which spelled out the issues we discussed in the previous chapter). On the other side, a document was drawn up and signed ultimately by nearly 1,300 ministers in the PCUSA stating that they affirmed the Westminster Standards and the basic beliefs of the five fundamental doctrines, but they also said the following:

We are united in believing that these are not the only theories allowed by the Scriptures and our standards as explanations of these facts and doctrines of our religion, and that all who hold to these facts and doctrines, whatever theories they may employ to explain them, are worthy of all confidence and fellowship.

This declaration became known as the Auburn Affirmation because the original document was first circulated by a professor at the Auburn (NY) Theological Seminary. It, along with Union Seminary in New York Seminary, was the training ground for most of the Liberals in the PCUSA. The full statement of the Auburn Affirmation is contained in Appendix C.

The signers of this declaration also asserted that requiring subscription to the fundamental five doctrines was unconstitutional. This position was debated not just on the floor of presbytery and General Assembly meetings, but also in the front pages of major metropolitan daily newspapers.

At the 1924 General Assembly, a conservative minister from Philadelphia was elected as Moderator. At the end of the meeting the Assembly however, he refused to act on a number of overtures seeking to declare the Auburn Affirmation heretical and schismatic. Strangely, there was not even one protest filed or one dissenting vote recorded in regard to the recommendation of the Bills and Overtures Committee to take no action.

In twelve months time, something radical, something historic, had clearly happened. Here is what Dr. Gordon Clark, long time Head of the Philosophy Department at Butler University and a former ruling elder in the PCUSA (and later a teaching elder in the Orthodox Presbyterian Church and Reformed Presbyterian Church Evangelical Synod) said by way of analysis of what happened:

> When future historians of the Church evaluate this present age, the publication of the Auburn Affirmation will stand out in importance like Luther's nailing his ninety-five theses. But it will be important for a different reason. The reason the Auburn Affirmation is so important is that it constitutes a major offensive against the Word of God. It, or at least its theology, is the root of Presbyterian apostasy.

The battle continued until 1927. The conservatives held that the issue at stake was that the five Fundamentals under consideration were in fact five doctrines, which are clearly taught in the Bible and they were essential to any system of doctrine which calls itself Christian, whether it be Reformed, or broadly Protestant, or even Catholic. The final response of the General Assembly was that requiring subscription to the fundamental five doctrines was unconstitutional, saying that they could not categorically declare *any* doctrines as "essential and necessary."

At the same time all of this was going on, there grew up a crisis in the administration of Princeton Seminary. For many years, there were two distinct boards in control of the seminary. The Board of Trustees held control of the property and the Faculty board held control of all educational matters. In 1822, a Board of Directors was created, under the General Assembly, but their role was very passive, simply making recommendations for faculty hires. In fact, it was not until 1902 that there was even a President elected—the faculty would simply elect a Chairman. In 1902, Dr. Francis Patton retired as President of Princeton College and was elected President of the Seminary by the Board of Directors mostly as an honorary position. Patton carried out his duties in a way similar to the Chairman of the Faculty rather than in the way you and I would understand what the president of an educational intuition would do today. However, upon Patton's retirement in 1913, a search was made for a new President and the Board of Directors elected a prominent pastor from Baltimore, J. Ross Stevenson to the office. He was inaugurated in 1914.

Immediately Stevenson took on the roll of a very pro-active President, taking leadership not only in administration of the school, but having a major roll in selecting new faculty. Stevenson was elected by a majority of just one vote on the Board of Directors, which by this time was equally split between the growing division of liberals and conservatives.

From the outset, Stevenson had the theological support of only one faculty member—Charles Erdman. While being a leading evangelical writer (I personally came to trust in Jesus in 1969 while reading the Gospel of John and a small commentary written by Erdman on the Gospel), Erdman held to an inclusive view of the church. Stevenson wanted to change the makeup of the faculty to include all theological views in the church, while the majority of the faculty was insistent they remain consistent to their Old School heritage and to the confessional standards of the church.

During Stevenson's tenure, several major events evidenced the conflict. In 1924, following the refusal of the General Assembly to declare the Auburn Affirmation as heretical, a group of students at Princeton Seminary joined a League of Evangelical Students, distinctly separate from the official seminary Student Association. Stevenson wanted the group disbanded but the Faculty supported and maintained their existence.

In 1925, the official student association president, acting in the traditional way, asked Dr. Charles Erdman to continue for his 21$^{st}$ year as Faculty advisor. But when the entire student association cabinet met for the first time, they voted to withdraw the invitation offered by their president to Erdman and asked the Faculty to appoint the advisor. The faculty then elected Robert Dick Wilson, a clear conservative. Stevenson was furious.

In 1926, the Faculty voted to recommend that Machen be elected to the Chair of Apologetics at the Seminary, but that needed confirmation by the General Assembly. At the Assembly, Stevenson and Erdman strongly opposed this appointment and the Assembly took no action on the recommendation, thus denying the position to Machen.

The next year, there was a flare-up between Erdman and Machen after Erdman's election to the pulpit at First Church, Princeton (where Machen had previously served because it was the church's policy to call a faculty member as their pastor). This flare-up took place on the pages of a denominational magazine and thus became quite public. So much so that in 1926, reacting to requests from the Board of Trustees and a minority of the Board of Directors to have the General Assembly investigate problems at the Seminary, the General Assembly appointed a five-man committee. Their instructions were to "make a sympathetic study of conditions affecting the welfare of Princeton Seminary and to cooperate responsively with seminary leaders in striving to adjust and harmonize differences, and to report to the next Assembly."

The following year this committee reported that. "the root and source of the serious difficulties at Princeton and the greatest obstacle to the removal of these difficulties, seem to be in the plan of government by two boards." Accordingly, the Assembly set out to change the government of the seminary and appointed a different study committee. At the 1929 General Assembly the study committee presented a majority report to unite the work of the two boards into one, proceeding to the election of a new board which would consist of one-third each from the current two boards and one-third at large from the Assembly. A minority report was presented by a relative of B. B. Warfield, supported by a petition signed by over 10,000 teaching and ruling elders within the PCUSA. Despite this strong minority opinion, the Assembly proceeded to elect the new, single board and even included two men who had signed the Auburn Affirmation as part of the at-large portion.

The leading conservative on the Board of Directors, the Reverend Clarence McCartney of Philadelphia, refused to serve on the new board, and four of the most conservative professors at Princeton—Machen, Robert Dick Wilson, Oswald T. Allis and Cornelius Van Til—resigned from the faculty. The days of the Princeton Theology had come to a close.

Again, all this conflict was being reported in the mainline newspapers of the day. In fact, the editorial page of the Boston Evening Transcript made these comments concerning the change at Princeton Seminary:

One cannot say what will happen at Princeton Theological Seminary, but one hopes that the house will stand. Clearly the battle at Princeton has a significance reaching far beyond its local scene. Its forces, its bitterness, give strong indication that the issues there in contest, as in other parts of the United States, are the dominant issues of the religious thought of our times. Certainly with regard to the Protestant denominations, it now seems clear that upon the outcome of the warfare, whether for weal or woe, the future character of Protestant Christianity depends.

The actions of the General Assembly of 1929 made it clear to many conservatives that there was a need for a new seminary to continue the Princeton Theology. One group met in New York City in June to discuss what to do. Another group met in mid-July in Philadelphia and it became clear there was enough critical mass in that city to proceed. On July 18, 1929 a public meeting was held at the YMCA in Philadelphia attended by more than seventy men, and plans were made to open the doors of the new Westminster Theological Seminary that fall.

The four former Princeton faculty members—Allis, Machen Van Til and Wilson were appointed as professors, with Wilson as Chairman. They were joined by three recent Princeton graduates who had lately completed doctoral studies, and a year later by John Murray who left the Princeton faculty to join them. They opened their doors in September with fifty students and with a Board of Trustees made up entirely of ministers and ruling elders in the PCUSA. The men who started this seminary were not in any way censored for starting an independent work. They continued to operate it within the framework of the denomination just as the Liberals operated the independent Union Seminary in New York.

Parallel with this crisis in the area of seminary education, a crisis was also developing in the area of foreign missions. While there was a systemic problem, two major incidents brought the crisis to the forefront.

In 1930, lay representatives of seven different denominations, including the PCUSA, met to convene a group who wanted to research and report on the effectiveness of foreign missions by American churches. They published their report, entitled "Rethinking Missions," in which they stated their objections to the traditional work of missions to plant specifically Christian churches and even the necessity of espousing Christianity for one to be in a right relationship with God. They recommended cooperation with and accommodation of non-Christian religions in the various mission fields.

While the Missions Board of the PCUSA made a formal disclaimer against this report, it became apparent that those principles were already being applied on some mission fields—especially in China through the work of a Presbyterian missionary named Pearl Buck. Mrs. Buck was a famous anthropologist and well-read novelist. She was working in China, primarily teaching at Nanking University. Pearl had been raised in China by Presbyterian missionaries, was married to another Presbyterian missionary and was known universally herself as a missionary. However, her writings made it crystal clear that she had no use for the Christian gospel.

In May of 1933, Dr. Machen wrote an overture and submitted it to his presbytery (New Brunswick in New Jersey) asking for a reorganization of the Mission Board and clarification of these serious theological problems. It was denied by the presbytery. However, the same overture was later passed by the more conservative Philadelphia Presbytery and sent to the General Assembly—which promptly denied it.

This lack of action resulted in Machen and as many as nine other PCUSA ministers forming the Independent Board for Presbyterian Foreign Missions with a purpose to promote "purely biblical and Presbyterian missions." The next year the General Assembly adopted a resolution that commanded the Independent Board to cease soliciting funds within the PCUSA and demanded that the ministers of the church resign from the Board or suffer discipline. None did.

Machen, who was serving as President of the Board, was the first one to come under discipline and he was suspended from office in 1935. Philadelphia Presbytery, although theologically conservative, was still an Old School Presbytery and believed in a strict application of discipline. They suspended their four ministers on the grounds that working with an Independent Board was contrary to Presbyterian polity. In an unusual turn of events, the more theological liberal New York Presbytery failed to discipline the one member of the Independent Board among their membership.

All of the suspensions were appealed to the 1936 General Assembly, and when they were all upheld, the formation of a new denomination was inevitable. On June 11, 1936, 34 ministers, 17 ruling elders and 79 laymen met in Philadelphia to form the Presbyterian Church *of* America (PCofA). In the next chapter, we will trace the sad course of the "Split P's" in that small struggling group.

## Chapter Fourteen
## "I've Been an OP, BP, EPC and an RPCES" –
## The "Split P's"

I make no apologies in telling you up front that this chapter will be longer than most and contain some personal observations because my own spiritual roots come from within the progression of "Split P's" that gave rise to a song entitled "I've been an OP, BP, EPC, and RPCES—and what I'll be this time next year is anybody's guess!" (We'll learn more about that song in Chapter Seventeen!)

In the first few years of the PCofA, this new conservative denomination suffered some severe blows, not the least of which was the death of the one man most responsible for the founding of the group, Dr. J. Gresham Machen. We must take time to learn a bit more about him.

Machen had Southern Presbyterian roots. He received a BA at Johns Hopkins in 1901 and then an MA and BD at Princeton in 1904 and 1905. From there he went to Germany to pursue doctoral studies. We have already heard in the last chapter of his role in leaving Princeton to start Westminster Seminary, as well as his role on the Independent Board of Presbyterian Foreign Missions.

Machen was also a famous author. He wrote a New Testament grammar that is still in use today in some quarters. In 1921, he published a book entitled *The Origin of Paul's Religion* which was his answer to the "comparative religion" branch of Liberalism of the day. In 1930, he published a book on the *Virgin Birth of Christ* that may have been his most scholarly work. And of course, he wrote *Christianity and Liberalism* which we have already examined.

When the PCofA held its 1st General Assembly in June of 1936, Machen was elected as the first Moderator. An interesting sidelight worth noting is that—following the tradition that a newly-elected Moderator is escorted to the chair by members of the court; the two men who escorted Machen were the Reverend Carl McIntire and Dr. J. Oliver Buswell, Jr. (more on them later).

The 2nd General Assembly was held just a few months later in November of 1936 in order to adopt a constitution. But it was at the 3rd General Assembly that the PCofA ran into big problems. To begin with, Dr. Machen had died in January of 1937 while he was traveling on a denomination organizational trip. John Muether, the Orthodox Presbyterian Church historian, tells the story of his death in his *This Week in the OPC* (taken from the denominational web site):

> During the Christmas recess at Westminster Theological Seminary, Machen agreed to travel to North Dakota to speak at some of the churches in the six-month old denomination that he had helped to found. He took ill during the trip but insisted on fulfilling his obligations when he arrived in the twenty-degree-below-zero weather. After speaking in Leith and then in Bismarck, his condition worsened to the point where he was hospitalized for pneumonia.
>
> In *J. Gresham Machen: A Biographical Memoir*, Ned B. Stonehouse records Machen's death in this way: "On New Year's Eve Mr. [Samuel J.] Allen called briefly and offered prayer. And then Machen told him of a vision he had had of being in heaven: 'Sam, it was glorious, it was

glorious.' And a little later, 'Sam, isn't the Reformed Faith grand?' The following day he was largely unconscious, but there were intervals when his mind was thoroughly alert. In one of those periods he dictated a telegram to his colleague John Murray which was his final word: 'I'm so thankful for the active obedience of Christ. No hope without it.' And so he died at about 7:30 p.m. on January 1, 1937."

With Machen gone, there was an immediate void in the leadership of the PCofA, and three issues had grown by this time to inflammable levels. The first of the three major areas of controversy involved those in the new group who held strong pre-millennial views and their charge that their positions were not truly allowed to be held, and in fact were being attacked in many fronts.

Two presbyteries overtured the General Assembly asking that some declaration be adopted, stating that there was "eschatological liberty" in the church. The Assembly did not adopt such a declaration because the majority of members believed that such liberty already existed within the doctrinal standard and constitution of the church—at least for historic pre-millenialism—but certainly not for the pre-tribulation rapture brand that had become so popular among dispensationalists in the 20th Century.

The second area of controversy was one of Christian liberties. Many accused the new denomination and the seminary in particular of promoting the use of alcohol and tobacco. This issue came to a climax at the 3rd General Assembly, when overtures relative to total abstinence were defeated and an overture was adopted directing the attention of the church to the Westminster Standards as containing sufficient and adequate instruction on this subject. (There is, after all, an entire chapter on the subject in the Confession.)

A third area also came to a head at this same Assembly, when it passed a resolution urging the church not to continue to support the Independent Board of Presbyterian Foreign Missions—which had been founded by many of their leaders during their final years in the PCUSA. The proponents of this resolution claimed that since the Independent Board was now headed by a man who was not even in a Presbyterian church, it had ceased fulfilling its original purpose of being "truly biblical and truly Presbyterian."

As a result of these differences, fourteen ministers and three ruling elders walked out of the meeting and withdrew from the denomination forming yet a different group known as the Bible Presbyterian Synod. It primarily included the pre-millenialists; the proponents of abstinence; and the separatists willing to work with like-minded, non-Presbyterian separatists. Along with this new denomination, a new Seminary, named Faith Theological Seminary, was established at Wilmington, Delaware. Members of this group represented, for the most part, those who lost the votes in all three of the areas of controversy described above.

The remaining PCofA after the 1937 split slowly began to grow as many people left their home churches to join the cause. As the economy grew tighter and tighter because money was poured into the economic buildup for World War II, the people were forced to sacrifice to do whatever it took to form new churches.

Again, looking to John Muether for help, we discover when and how the name of the fledgling denomination was changed.

Threatened by a lawsuit by the Presbyterian Church in the U. S. A., the young church determined at the Fifth General Assembly in 1939 that it lacked the financial resources necessary to sustain the legal challenge to its name. Commissioners to that Assembly chose the new name after a vigorous, twelve-hour debate. Other names considered were the Evangelical Presbyterian Church, the Presbyterian and Reformed Church of America, the North American Presbyterian Church, the American Presbyterian Church, the Presbyterian Church of Christ, the Protestant Presbyterian Church of America, the Seceding Presbyterian Church (of America), the Free Presbyterian Church of America, the American Orthodox Presbyterian Church, and the True Presbyterian Church of the World.

Historian Mark Noll interpreted the debate in this way: "In the end sentiment was divided nearly equally between the Orthodox Presbyterian Church and the Evangelical Presbyterian Church, with only lesser support for names retaining the word 'America.' By just one vote 'Orthodox' prevailed over 'Evangelical,' and so it has remained to this day. Most significantly, the new name indicated a new perspective. No longer would the denomination aspire to be *the* Presbyterian Church of America." Which is ultimately one of the reason's today's PCA uses the pronoun 'in'.

The OPC remains today as a viable denomination with a slow and steady growth rate, but it is one that is very reluctant to merge with any other similar group. We will see more of this in the story of Joining and Receiving in Chapter Seventeen.

We turn back now to the history of the Bible Presbyterian Synod—those who walked out of the OPC in 1937. This group continued to grow at a steady pace for eighteen years. The clear leader of the group was the Reverend Carl McIntire, pastor of the large Collingswood (NJ) Bible Presbytery Church. (Rev. McIntire, you will recall, was one of those men who escorted Machen to the moderator's chair at the 1st General Assembly of the PCofA). McIntire graduated from Westminster Seminary in 1931, being one of the students who left Princeton. He became pastor of the Collingswood Church in 1933. McIntire was among the founding members of the Independent Board for Presbyterian Foreign Missions and was one of the men suspended by the PCUSA in 1935. McIntire joined Machen and others in the Presbyterian Church of America in the summer of 1936.

When the new denomination was immediately beset with arguments over the issues we have just discussed, McIntire led those who left to form the Bible Presbyterian Church. Within this newest group, McIntire's church was easily the largest, with some 1,200 members. This support base allowed for a diverse number of ministries, including the publication entitled *The Christian Beacon* which began in 1936 and which operated as a journal of record for the Bible Presbyterian Church for many years. In 1937, McIntire founded Faith Theological Seminary, aided in part by the assistance of then-student Francis A. Schaeffer.

By the start of American involvement in World War II in 1941, McIntire had seen the need to get Bible-believing men into the military chaplaincy. The American Council of Christian Churches (ACCC) was started to represent biblically conservative churches as well as to act as a counterpart to the larger, but clearly liberal, National Council of Churches and World Council of Churches.

As the chaplaincy was then run on a quota system, McIntire worked to increase the numbers of people represented by the American Council. His success in this work allowed many conservatives into the chaplaincy, but this same success later led to excess, and by 1955, the Bible Presbyterian Church was in turmoil over charges that McIntire was inflating the membership numbers of the Council. Those charges were leveled by Francis Schaeffer and Robert G. Rayburn (then President of Highland College, a BPC institution in Glendale, California) among others.

At the BPC Synod of 1954 in Greenville, SC, the issue of Dr. McIntire's ethics was raised publicly by Bob Rayburn. No vote was taken that year to discipline McIntire; however, a protest was approved by the Assembly and sent to the American Council concerning their actions.

The next year at the Synod of 1955, held at the Covenant Presbyterian Church in St. Louis, the schism came. I first heard the story of this meeting from my mentor and Church history professor, Will Barker, who grew up in the Covenant Church and was home on vacation from Princeton University where he was a student that year. Thus, he attended the proceedings.

The first report was by Dr. Rayburn, that there had been no response from the American Council on the protest sent to them the previous year (which should not be surprising since McIntire pretty much ran the organization through his personal power and influence). A vote was then taken by the BPC Synod to withdraw from the ACCC and it passed by a significant majority. Immediately following the vote, McIntire and his associates stormed out of the church in a tirade and gathered in the shade of several large trees in front of the sanctuary building. They immediately set plans to meet at

McIntire's church in 1956 to continue the Bible Presbyterian Church. About forty percent of the denomination followed McIntire's leadership.

As an interesting aside, by the time Dr. Rayburn had returned the next week to the college in California, where he served as President, he discovered that all the locks on the doors—including to his own office—had been changed. The majority of Trustees of the college were McIntire supporters!

RPCES minister George Hutchinson, in his excellent work *The History Behind the Reformed Presbyterian Church, Evangelical Synod* (Mack, Cherry Hill, NJ, 1974) gives his analysis of what had happened in the previous two decades. (By the way, I am indebted to Hutchinson's work for providing the outline for much of the rest of this chapter.)

It may be the case that the chief problem facing the Bible Presbyterian Church throughout its history was bigger than Carl McIntire, though no doubt emboldened by him. Could it have been the subtle spirit of "movementism," which from the nature of the case, endangered the Presbyterian Separatist Movement from the beginning?

The mentality of "movementism" involves dedication to what is held to be a holy cause under divinely-appointed leadership, often narrowed down to one extremely gifted man. The movement is born in the midst of severe opposition and suffering but slowly gathers strength. All those who are on the right track will give themselves wholly to the movement in recognition of the rightness of the cause and the God-given character of its leadership.

As the movement progresses, a "movementistic" attitude is revealed when any deviation from the leadership is viewed as a compromising betrayal of the cause and provokes severe counter criticism. Significant differences of opinion are looked upon with suspicion, and more and more of the originally enthusiastic adherents are alienated from the movement until finally only the slavish followers of the leadership remain.

The seeds of the "movementistic" mentality, which from the nature of the case existed in the separatist movement from the beginning, were watered by the struggles of the 1930s. The subtle spirit of "movementism" may have endangered the ministry of Dr. Machen and his most loyal followers. There can be little doubt that movementism has vitiated the ministry of McIntire who has looked upon himself as Dr. Machen's successor.

With perfect Monday-morning quarterbacking ability, Hutchinson's theory proved itself correct in the history over the next forty years as McIntire again and again led splits to form smaller and smaller groups who would follow him.

Let me interject a personal story at this point that I believe shows how sad this episode of 20th Century Presbyterian history really was. I first heard the gospel and came to faith in Jesus under the ministry of the Reverend Howard Oakley, pastor of the Covenant Presbyterian Church in Cherry Hill, NJ. Howard had been led to the Lord by McIntire (so I guess that makes me one of Carl's spiritual grandsons!)

One Sunday night, while I was finishing my service in the Navy in the Philadelphia area waiting for discharge and going to seminary, I went to church at Collingswood. There were about 400 people in attendance—not bad for a Sunday evening service (even back in those days). This was 1970 and McIntire was involved in a lot of political activism, especially anti-communist rallies. Remember, this was long before Jerry Falwell and Pat Robertson got into the business of political activism. The announcements that evening took at least thirty or forty minutes to describe this upcoming rally, and that bus trip to picket, and what have you.

About that time, a homeless man walked in to the rear of the sanctuary and Carl had the ushers bring the man up to the front pew. Carl came out of the pulpit, stood next to the man, introduced himself, welcomed him to the church, made a crisp, clear, winsome presentation of the gospel to him, and asked several deacons to take the man to a motel and provide for his needs.

By the time McIntire got back in the pulpit, he preached one of the finest sermons I have ever heard on Justification by Faith. But the problem was all the other stuff you had to sit through before hearing the preaching. As I walked out—and this was before I learned all the history we have just covered about the BPC—I knew my decision to go to Covenant Seminary in St. Louis was the right one. I certainly didn't belong in the BPC.

This makes an excellent transition back to the Bible Presbyterian Church, Columbus Synod. Recall, they were the sixty percent of remaining churches from the 1955 division. One of their leaders, the Reverend Kenneth Horner, wrote an unpublished personal analysis of the situation within that group at the time of the St. Louis split that is quoted by Hutchinson (p. 301). It is quite helpful:

In the midst of such disruption, there comes a great temptation to all to turn our backs upon the whole church and movement and go our own independent way or find another denomination with which to work. As I have personally faced this temptation and sought to think it through, I believe it would be most glorifying to God to remain with the church to which He led me at the beginning of my ministry and to trust Him to enable us to weather this storm. We never solve problems by running away from them; and as someone has wisely said, "When in a fog, throw out the anchor." It is very important to move slowly rather than precipitously these days, and we must therefore go ahead on our knees trusting the Lord to guide us.

(On a personal note, Horner's analysis is precisely why I continue to remain in the PCA today. It's where God called me to the ministry and it's where I am convinced he wants me to seek to do His work.)

It is clear that for the most part Horner's peers followed his advice—particularly as they tiptoed through the minefields of issues all around them. The biggest mine was, of course, that necessity to maintain personal and ecclesiastical separation from Modernism. That was essential for both groups of BP's.

The issue of Christian liberties, especially in the area of abstinence from alcohol and tobacco, was also high on their agenda although leaders such as Bob Rayburn now began to encourage balance in order to avoid extremism. Slowly but surely just about everyone came to understand—primarily through the leadership of R. Laird Harris and others—that the real enemy was Modernism in the church and not the growing powerful communist governments and societies all around them.

The Columbus branch of the BPC had to form all new agencies since the McIntire forces held control of the old ones. A new college, named Covenant College, was begun under the leadership of Bob Rayburn in California in 1955, but by the fall of 1956, it moved to St. Louis and began using space in the large Covenant Church.

Rayburn had been an Army Chaplain during WWII and then returned to the pastorate. In 1950, as he was serving as pastor of the (still) independent College Church in Wheaton, IL, he was recalled to active duty during the Korean War. The story of his reporting to his airborne unit in Korea just hours before they took off for a combat drop behind enemy lines and, despite the objections of his new Commanding Officer, actually participated in the combat jump without *any* previous parachute training is a legend still talked about in the Army Chaplain Corps.

At the same time the new seminary was formed, with Rayburn as President and with Dr. J. Oliver Buswell serving as the Dean (recall that he was the other man along with McIntire who escorted Machen to the Moderator chair in 1936).

Since the McIntire forces controlled the Independent Board of Presbyterian Foreign Missions, a new Presbyterian agency had to be formed and the task fell to the Reverend William Mahlow, Sr. Bill was a graduate of Faith Seminary and had served as a missionary in India from 1947 to 1952. He then served as General Secretary of the Independent Board for a time. He became the founding Executive Director of World Presbyterian Missions (the Columbus Synod's agency) in 1958 and led it through many years of growth until 1971, when he resigned to spend his full time with a church he had planted in Annapolis that grew so fast it needed his full-time attention.

The Home Missions (church planting) board went through a number of leaders. Tom Cross began with great evangelistic zeal but then decided he would rather do the actual planting rather than the administration, ending up planting a number of churches in the Greenville and Columbia, SC area. He was replaced by Jay Adams, whose theological precision and lack of sufficient funding slowed things down for a spell. Howard Oakley took the job for the while but it ultimately fell to Don MacNair, then pastor of the denomination's "mother" church (Covenant, St. Louis), to take over National Presbyterian Missions (NPM) in 1964 and build it up to be one of the most efficient and effective such agencies in the nation.

Even though I got one of my few "B" grades in seminary in MacNair's Church Planting Class, I was invited to be the organizing pastor of a new RPCES work starting in Atlanta in the fall of 1973, while I was still a student in St. Louis. (My wife Esther got an "A" in that class, and that was the only time she beat me with a grade in any class.) I would commute every week (fly down on Thursday, return on the red-eye late Sunday night) trying in a futile effort to start an RPCES congregation at the same time the PCA was forming. (Going head to head with the new PCA was probably not NPM's finest hour!)

Another major institution was begun during this period—although it was an independent one. In 1955, Francis Schaeffer, originally a close confidant of McIntire but parted with him at the time of the 1956 division, moved to Switzerland where he would establish a movement called L'Abri. To the minds of many (including me), Schaeffer was the finest Christian evangelist and apologist in the world in the last half of the 20th Century. If you have not yet read his story, you must. His wife, Edith, wrote the book, simply called *L'Abri*.

So influential was Schaeffer that in 1970 when I arrived to begin my studies at Covenant Seminary, nearly half of my new-student peers had come to seminary one way or another through the ministry of L'Abri. Can you just imagine a twelve-year Navy veteran enlisted man with short hair in the midst of a cross-cultural experience with late 60s hippies who had come to Jesus through Schaeffer's ministry? Another reason Covenant was the right choice for my seminary!

At the 25th Anniversary Synod of the Bible Presbyterian Church (Columbus Synod, which still viewed itself as the "true" BPC), the decision was made to change the name of the denomination. The confusion in trying to explain that they were not related to Carl McIntire and his political machinations caused so much confusion among the public in general and also the press that it had become just too much.

They picked the name Evangelical Presbyterian Church although some would have preferred a more distinct reference to the Reformed faith in the name. However, the growing desire to see the gospel spread in the world, when explained on the floor by great leaders such as Kyle Thurman, carried the day. (Recall the name EPC had failed by only one vote from becoming the name of the OPC.) Still, there remained a large degree of tension among those in the EPC who wanted to make the advance of the gospel the priority of the church's ministry against the (thinning) numbers who maintained that the church must condemn the social evils of the day in the prophetic tradition of ancient Israel.

R. Laird Harris—a great Old Testament scholar who could keep a class wide awake for fifty minutes talking about dinosaurs and the day-age theory of creation—gave a sound argument against the latter emphasis—writing in the May 1958 issue of the *Bible Presbyterian*. First, he pointed out, the ministry of the prophets was not simply to denounce sin, but to reveal to men the word of God. A prophet is not simply a synonym for a courageous preacher, but one who speaks the word of God by inspiration.

"Then we must remember," said Harris, "that the situation in our day is different from that in Israel's day. In ancient Israel, church and state were united in accordance with the command of God. However, today the situation is far different. By God's command, church and state are now separated so that the church has no rightful control over the state." Harris summarized:

The church's ministry is now wholly to the individual with a message of salvation and sanctification. The corporate church surely has no business lobbying in the halls of Congress for any specific program however laudable it may be. Today, the establishment of civil righteousness within the state and among the nations is in the civil powers. The state is supreme in civil matters; the church is supreme in the spiritual sphere. They should be kept separate.

But then Harris immediately added:

Christianity must affect every area of the life of Christians and make them live according to righteousness. This is a far different thing from making Christianity try to affect every individual in a nation and making the individual citizens live as Christians. They will not do so and they cannot! It is useless for the church to try to impose Christian standards of morality on a nation. To do so the church would have either to lower its standards or to impose a standard impossible for the nation to keep.

Harris's position began to carry the day in the EPC. This resulted in a shift from separatist form to biblical content in the work and worship of the church, with a more positive outward face shown to the world. The church began to express a balanced testimony.

Will Barker, by then ordained and serving as pastor of the EPC church in the St. Louis suburb of Hazelwood, wrote a series of articles in the denominational magazine *The Reporter*, in which he used an analogy between the EPC and the pre-Reformation group we learned of in Chapter One known as the Waldensians, the followers of Peter Waldo.

The desire of the EPC was for a thoroughly biblical Christianity to exist in America and this desire was much like the desire for a Reformation. However, since no such Reformation has taken place on the scale of that in the $16^{th}$ and $17^{th}$ Centuries, the EPC must be like the Waldensians, said Barker, i.e., see the issues clearly; maintain their distinctives, but exercise patience until God would bring about a full Reformation.

This was the state of the Evangelical Presbyterian Church when it decided to stop the ongoing series of "Split 'P's" and finally to merge with a smaller sister denomination—the Reformed Presbyterian Church, General Synod.

You may recall from Chapter Ten that the mainline Presbyterians (who came from the Church of Scotland) were not the only ones who had divided once they formed as a denomination in the United States. The same fate had befallen the Reformed Presbyterians who came from the Covenanters of Scotland and never were part of the mainline churches here in the U.S.

In 1833, that Reformed Presbyterian denomination divided into two groups—one known as the Reformed Presbyterian Church, General Synod, called the New Light Synod. The Old Light Synod was officially named the Reformed Presbyterian Church, Covenanter Synod. (As a reminder, this latter group remains intact yet today, as the Reformed Presbyterian Church in North America.)

In 1959, the divided portion known as the General Synod dropped their historical positions of adherence to Covenanter standards as part of their constitution, which was not so much a change in their theology as it was the bringing of their constitution in line with what had long been the practice in the denomination. Just prior to this change, and increasing even more afterwards, a number of men who desired to leave the mainline PCUSA (but who for various reasons did not want to be part of the Orthodox Presbyterian Church) decided that the RPC, General Synod was the proper place to move. One of the best-known names making that transfer was Dr. Gordon Clark.

These new men had close friendship and contacts with men who were in the Bible Presbyterian Church, Columbus Synod (now called the Evangelical Presbyterian Church) and so discussions quickly began with the RPC, General Synod concerning union. There had been tentative discussions before but nothing had come of those. This time the momentum was much stronger.

After several years of complicated negotiations of principles for union (too detailed for a book of this nature), discussions were held primarily on issues of eschatological freedom and living a "separated life." These led to a development of what was recognized as a middle ground between the OPC and EPC (recall these issues were crucial in that separation in 1937).

It should be pointed out that one of the reasons that so few negotiated mergers take place among the more conservative, Bible-believing denominations may well be that they take their principles very seriously. It was those principles that had caused them to divide in the first place. It would be much more simple for two more liberal groups (within the same general faith group) to merge because in many cases they would not have many strong principles that require negotiation.

Finally, in 1964 after several years of fits and starts and delays and feet-dragging, a Plan of Union was finally approved by both denominations and in April of 1965 both denominations held their Synod meetings simultaneously on the campus of Covenant College on top of Lookout Mountain (just over the Tennessee line in Georgia).

The 142$^{nd}$ meeting of the General Synod of the RPC met first and unanimously approved the union. Then the 29$^{th}$ Synod of the EPC voted to approve the merger. A uniting service was held at 10:00 a.m. on that April 6$^{th}$ day. Dr. J. Oliver Buswell, Jr. led the combined group in the prayer of dedication. (Once again, recall that he was one of the men who escorted Machen to the Moderator's chair in 1936!)

In picking a name, they also merged pieces of each group's name, calling the new denomination the Reformed Presbyterian Church, Evangelical Synod. Notice the deference given to the RP side of the merger which, although much smaller in size, was very strong in heritage. This heritage was celebrated by continuing the numbering of Synods of the new merged group, picking up with the 143$^{rd}$ Synod as the number of the first merged synod meeting.

At last, the slide into split after split had slowed down in the North although there would still be several additional fractures from the mainline denomination in the next thirty years (continuing even today). Among the "Split P's" however, the momentum had clearly changed. We will see this momentum come to full fruition after we pause for the next two chapters to examine the somewhat-later-in-time but similar decline in the Southern Presbyterian Church and the major division that formed the Presbyterian Church in America.

The next two chapters were written by two men who are far more knowledgeable about these issues than I will ever be, and they among those who were active in forming the PCA. I entered seminary from a "Split P" church (Reformed Presbyterian Church, Evangelical Synod). Thus, I spent many hours learning the northern Presbytery history. But while I was ordained in the PCA (actually it was called the National Presbyterian Church at that time), I was not present at the 1st General Assembly of the PCA.

The next chapter on Southern Presbyterian Roots was written by Dr. Morton Smith, a noted professor of theology and historian who served as the first Stated Clerk of the PCA. The material presented is based on a lecture delivered on July 31, 2005 to the adult Sunday school class of Westminster Presbyterian Church, Roanoke Virginia, by Dr. Morton Smith. It has been adapted by permission for use in this work.

The chapter following that one, was written by Dr. Charles Dunahoo, who has served since 1977 as the Coordinator of the PCA's Christian Education and Publications Committee. and was a member of the Executive Committee of the Organizing Committee that did the primary organization for the formation of a new denomination, now known as the PCA. The material in that chapter is based on a lecture delivered on August 6, 2005 to the adult Sunday school class of Westminster Presbyterian Church, Roanoke Virginia. The lecture notes have been adapted by permission for use in this work.

## Chapter Fifteen
## The Southern Presbyterian Roots of the PCA

Since the PCA was, at its outset, a separation from the Southern Presbyterian Church, this chapter of necessity will have a bit more detail than some of the previous ones. Some information was contained in Chapter Ten on early Presbyterian history in America, and in Chapter Thirteen on the Old School/New School divisions of the Northern Presbyterian Church, but we will amplify some of that a bit as well.

The Southern Presbyterian Church resided in the southern states that comprised the former Confederate States of America, plus the border states of Maryland, Kentucky and Missouri. The Southland was first settled in three different regions.

The first settlement of this area by Europeans was the Chesapeake society, beginning at Jamestown, Virginia (1607), which was the first permanent English colony in North America. Jamestown was settled by a Puritan company, and thus the first preachers in the colony there were of the Puritan viewpoint. There were some Presbyterian dissenters settled around the Norfolk area, but no permanent establishment of a Presbyterian church resulted there. Francis Makemie started out in this area when he arrived in 1680, before moving to join the Philadelphia Presbytery, (you will recall that name from Chapter Ten).

The second southern society was an entirely different settlement that took place in what may be called the Carolina lowlands, with Charleston, South Carolina, founded in 1670, as the central city. A whole colony of New Englanders moved to

South Carolina to establish a Congregational Church at Dorchester in 1696. Between 1752 and 1771, much of this group transplanted itself to Liberty County, Georgia, and established Midway Church there. From this Congregational church, a large number of young men were fed into the ministry of the Presbyterian Church. There were several attempts to form presbyteries in the low country but each of them failed.

Presbyterians also settled in the coastal areas of Georgia. As early as 1735, a number of Scottish Highlanders settled in Darien, Georgia. This was a community somewhat inland from Savannah, and served as a defense against the Spanish and the Indians. A Presbyterian Church was established there. At Savannah a number of Scots, Scots-Irish, French and Swiss Calvinists joined together in 1755 to form the Independent Meeting in Savannah, which continues to this day as the Independent Presbyterian Church of Savannah (which currently has a PCA pastor!)

The independency of spirit reflected in the Charleston-Savannah area has been characteristic of much Southern thought. Though it was forced on the early Presbyterians of this southern region by their distance from the rest of the American Presbyterians, it was to leave a mark on the South Carolina Presbyterian mind.

A number of highland Scots settled the Cape Fear River area of North Carolina in 1732. Scottish Presbyterianism was thus established in this region. By the time of the American War for Independence, 12,000 Highlanders were in this area. It was the largest Highlander settlement in the colonies. Their first minister was James Campbell, who came to Cross Creek from Pennsylvania in 1757. He first identified with the Presbytery of Charleston, but due to his inability to attend their meetings transferred to Orange Presbytery in North Carolina.

The fact that most of the Highlanders spoke only Gaelic (which continued to be used in some of the churches until after the War Between the States) protected them from the nearby Baptist missionaries at Sandy Creek and kept them faithful to Presbyterian Calvinism during the many years when they were without the ministrations of a regular pastor.

A third and somewhat later development was what is known as the backcountry of the South. It stretched from the Potomac, south to Georgia along the Appalachian chain of mountains, including the Virginia piedmont to the east of the Blue Ridge from Charlottesville south, the Valley of Virginia (which lies between the Blue Ridge and the Allegheny Mountains) and East Tennessee (which lies west of the first range of the Appalachians). In the Valley of Virginia, the Scots-Irish settled from Augusta County south to Big Lick (Roanoke). From there the stream of settlers divided, with many going southward into the piedmont area of North Carolina, and then westward along the foot of the mountains into South Carolina and Georgia. The other stream proceeded southwesterly through what is now southwest Virginia into east Tennessee. With them came the Presbyterian Church into both of these regions. Included in these Scots-Irish streams were the ancestors of Andrew Jackson, John C. Calhoun and Abraham Lincoln.

Among the early Presbyterian settlers in the Valley of Virginia was a group of Scots-Irish settlers from the Philadelphia area. In 1736, the Opequon Church, near Winchester, VA, was established which many believe is the oldest existing church of a continuous history in the Southern Presbyterian Church.

The division in 1741 between the Old Side and the New Side groups (which we covered in Chapter Ten) resulted in both denominations planting churches in the South. The Old

Side Church sent four ministers to establish churches in the Augusta County area of Virginia. The New Side Church. which had established a training academy in Pequa, PA, sent two ministers to Virginia, Samuel Stanhope Smith and John Blair Smith (both sons of the head of that academy). They became the first and second presidents of Hampden Sidney College near Farmville, Virginia.

In 1743, a Presbyterian minister named William Robinson visited in the Hanover County region of Virginia (near present-day Richmond) and preached a series of sermons. This turned out to be a momentous visit. Before this, missionary activities of the Presbyterian Church had been confined to Presbyterian communities. In Hanover, however, Presbyterianism entered upon a larger work; it was the first church to bring the revival and so to break the hold of the Anglican/Episcopalian Establishment in eastern Virginia.

Samuel Davies came to Hanover in 1747. Davies is often called the "Father of Southern Presbyterianism," since his labors brought about the establishment of the mother presbytery of the South, Hanover Presbytery. His first act was to go to Williamsburg, and receive a license to preach in four registered meeting places from Governor Gooch. This was in accord with the British Act of Toleration, which allowed dissenters to worship according to their consciences, so long as they did not disturb the peace and were loyal to the crown. Davies labored in Virginia from 1747 to 1759, and convened the first meeting of the Presbytery of Hanover on December 3, 1755, at the direction of the New Side Synod. The effect of his ministry was spread over all of Virginia and North Carolina.

During his sojourn in Virginia, he was able to get recognition of Presbyterian dissenters, which eventually broke the hold of the established Church in the eastern part of the colony. Davies spent much time working with the slaves. They made up a quarter to a third of his several congregations.

John Blair, the brother of Samuel Blair, served as acting president of the College of New Jersey (Princeton) until John Witherspoon came from Scotland. In 1746, John Blair visited the Valley of Virginia and organized the churches that became the nucleus of Lexington Presbytery. It was out of these churches that Liberty Hall Academy in Lexington, the predecessor of Washington College (now Washington and Lee University), was to come.

William Graham was the first teacher at the Academy. As we pointed out in Chapter Ten, he taught theology to Archibald Alexander, the founding professor of Princeton Theological Seminary. Others, who received their theological training from him, were Moses Hoge, John Holt Rice and George Addison Baxter. Hoge was the first professor of theology at Hampden Sydney, under Hanover Presbytery from 1807-1812, and appointed by the Synod of Virginia in 1812. Rice succeeded him, and founded Union Seminary in 1824. Baxter was professor of theology there at the time of the Old School-New School division of 1837.

Southern Presbyterianism, as it was first established, was warmly evangelical, on the one hand, and thoroughly orthodox in doctrine, on the other. In general, this marked the Southern Church until its decline into Liberalism in the 1950s and 1960s. There was zeal to spread the gospel of Christ for the saving of souls for all eternity, along with the desire to plant a church that was true to the Bible in all her doctrines and practices. This kind of Presbyterianism was what the Continuing Church Movement desired to preserve in launching the PCA.

We want to shift gears now and pick up with more details from Chapter Thirteen where we discussed the Northern

Church both before and after the War Between the States. You will recall that as a result of passing of the Spring Resolutions in the Old School Assembly, the Southern churches withdrew and joined with the New School Churches in the South to form what we refer to as the Southern Presbyterian Church.

The 1$^{st}$ Southern Presbyterian General Assembly was held at the First Presbyterian Church of Augusta, GA, on December 4, 1861. Dr. Benjamin Morgan Palmer, the Pastor of the First Presbyterian Church of New Orleans, preached the opening sermon on the Kingship of Christ. He was elected the first Moderator of the Southern Assembly.

A number of important theologians and churchmen in the Southern Church are still well known today. James Henley Thornwell was a dominant influence at the 1$^{st}$ Assembly. He was one of the greatest of the Southern Presbyterian theologians. Mr. Thornwell was the primary author of the "Address to all Churches" stating the reason for the rise of a new denomination, and setting forth the goals of the new church. Dr. Thornwell died in 1862, and thus did not have the ongoing impact on the developing church that he might have had if he had lived longer.

He was eventually succeeded at Columbia Theological Seminary by Dr. John L. Girardeau. Dr. Girardeau was one of the most eloquent preachers in South Carolina. Prior to the war, he spent much of his ministry with a black congregation in Charleston.

Dr. Robert L. Dabney was the leading theologian at Union Seminary, which was then located at Hampden Sydney. He continued to have a major influence on the Southern Church until his death in 1902.

Dr. B. M. Palmer, first Moderator of the Southern Assembly, returned to New Orleans after the war, and was a model pastor and preacher in that city for over forty years.

After the union of the Northern Old and New School groups in 1869, which essentially allowed both views in the united church, the Southern Church saw itself as the only remaining Old School Presbyterian Church. This is evident by the response of the Southern Presbyterian Church in 1870, to invitations to enter into correspondence with the view of their uniting with the Northern Church. The Southern Church answered in part with the following statement:

The union now consummated between the Old and New School Assemblies North was accomplished by methods, which, in our judgment, involved a total surrender of all the great testimonies of the Church for the fundamental doctrines of grace, at a time when the victory of truth over error hung long in the balance. The united Assembly stands of necessity upon an allowed latitude of interpretation of the Standards and must come at length to embrace nearly all shades of doctrinal belief. Of those falling testimonies we, are now the sole surviving heir, which we must lift from the dust and bear to the generations after us. It would be a serious compromise of this sacred trust to enter into public and official fellowship with those repudiating these testimonies and to do this expressly upon the ground as stated in the Preamble to the Overture before us, "that the terms of reunion between the two branches of the Presbyterian Church at the North, now happily consummated, present an auspicious opportunity for the adjustment of such relations." To found a correspondence professedly upon this idea would be to endorse that which we thoroughly disapprove.

From this quotation, it is obvious that the Southern Presbyterian Church in 1870 saw itself as the true continuing body of the Old School Presbyterian Church that had come into being in 1837. This then is the heritage of the Southern Presbyterian Church (or the Presbyterian Church in the United States as it had become officially known). This is the position that motivated the vast majority of men who were involved in the initial founding of the PCA.

Thomas Cary Johnson, who served as Professor of Ecclesiastical History and Polity (1892-1913), and later as Professor of Systematic Theology (1913-1930), at Union Theological Seminary of Virginia, wrote an article regarding the Southern Presbyterian Church, which appeared in the first bulletin of the Presbyterian Historical Society in 1901. He indicated that the Church had not moved away from her original stance forty years after her founding. "In doctrine the Church's movement has been, if any, to a more thorough-going Calvinism. No changes had occurred in the Confession or Catechisms except in a single paragraph about marriage with a deceased wife's sister." ("The Presbyterian Church in the United States," Journal of the Presbyterian Historical Society, I, 1902, p. 80.)

Johnson listed six distinctives of the PCUS, as it existed at the beginning of the 20th Century. To get something of the flavor of Southern Presbyterianism, we will examine the first four on this list.

1. The Southern Presbyterian Church was committed to the "plenary verbal inspiration" of the Bible, believing that this is the view, which the Bible teaches about itself. Her views touching the inerrancy of Scripture were not affected by the findings of biblical criticism. Inerrancy became one of the points of attack by the liberals as the Southern Church came under the influence of Liberalism. (Dr. Morton Smith notes that the

establishment of Reformed Theological Seminary in Jackson, MS was due to the fact that the four Southern Seminary presidents all agreed that they did not teach the inerrancy view of Scripture.)

2. One of the most prominent characteristics of the Southern Presbyterian Church was her jealous loyalty to the Westminster Standards. She held with unwavering firmness to the undiluted Calvinism of those Standards. As an Old School Church, she was committed to full subscription to the Standards. She saw no need of any new statement of old truth, but continued to be satisfied with the statement furnished by the heroic and Godly men of the 17th Century. (Again, Dr. Smith notes that as Liberalism took over the Southern Presbyterian Church in the 1940s and 1950s, Calvinism was all but lost in the South. Indeed, in the early 1950s there was only one member of the faculty of Columbia Theological Seminary—the most conservative of the Southern seminaries—who was a thoroughgoing Calvinist.)

3. The Southern Presbyterian Church held to the spirituality of the church, both in theory and in practice. The only task given to the church is that given by Christ in his Great Commission, namely, evangelism and nurture of her members. The Southern Church stressed the principle that "synods and councils are to handle, or conclude nothing but that which is ecclesiastical, and is not to intermeddle with civil affairs."

4. One of the major contributions of the Southern Presbyterian Church was in the area of polity. The Southern Presbyterian Church held a solid conviction of the *jure divino* (divine law) character of Presbyterianism. She developed an ecclesiastical polity that was distinguished for its constitutionality, particularly as seen in the complete parity of the ruling elders with teaching elders, the carefully defined

spheres and rights of the several courts, and its opposition to centralization of power.

Under the teaching of John L. Girardeau of Columbia Seminary, the office of deacon was expanded in the Southern Church. He saw the office as one to handle not just the ministry of mercy, but also other temporal affairs of the church. Thus, the Southern Presbyterians did not set up Trustees to handle the church property, but placed this under the care of the deacons. All too often in the Southern Church approach, the *only* function of the deacons was the care of property, and the ministry of mercy was neglected in far too many cases.

One other Southern Presbyterian distinctive in polity was the use of Assembly committees and not boards. Thornwell argued that the church did not have the right to erect any agency not provided in the Scriptures. A board, which could act on its own in carrying out the work of the Church, was considered such an unauthorized agent. Thus, the Southern Church appointed committees to assist the church in her work. The difference between committees and boards lies in the fact that committees are appointed to carry out specifically the task assigned to them by the Assembly, whereas a board is generally given much larger powers to act in a general area. Boards do not need to get permission to do some new function in their general area of operation, while a committee must have the task assigned to it.

The Southern Presbyterian Church remained essentially sound up to the 1930s. The conservative wing of the church controlled the General Assembly until 1939. The liberals (probably more from the neo-orthodox wing than the historical critical wing of liberals we discussed and defined in Chapter Twelve) gradually took control of the educational institutions, and the Christian Education and Publications Committee. Despite the conservative control of the church courts, the church failed to exercise discipline to remove those who were teaching error.

One of the leading liberals was Ernest Trice Thompson, who began teaching at Union Theological Seminary in Richmond in the 1920s. On the occasion of his retirement, he was praised for having broken all of the distinctives we have just discussed. As the liberals gained control of the church courts, and of the boards and agencies of the church, the conservatives found themselves always fighting a losing, defensive battle. It is important to understand how the departure came about in each of these four distinctives.

First, with regard to the high view of Scripture as the "only infallible rule of faith and practice," a lowered view of Scripture began to be found in the faculties of the seminaries as early as the 20s and 30s. For example, Ernest Trice Thompson was at Union Seminary as early as 1923. He openly endorsed the historical, critical approach to the Bible. He was moved from the Biblical Department to Church History and Polity, where he remained until his retirement in 1964. Despite this change in assignment, during his fifty years of teaching, he had taught over half of all the Southern Presbyterian ministers. Not all would have agreed with him, but he influenced a great many in the more liberal view.

In a history of the PCUS written by Thompson himself near the end of his career, he cites the fact that each of the other seminaries supported by the Southern Presbyterian Church moved at about this same time to the acceptance of the higher critical approach to Scripture. In fact, he accuses the new, independent Reformed Theological Seminary in Jackson, MS of having been formed in reaction to this trend in the denominational seminaries. He lists three distinctives and commitments of RTS. The first is to the "'plenary, verbal inspiration' of the Bible and 'its absolute inerrancy as the divinely revealed and authoritative Word of God.'" The second is to "the sovereignty of God as a central tenet of biblical faith, along with the related doctrines of absolute predestination and unconditional election." And the third is to "strict creedal subscription to the whole Reformed faith."

The second of the Southern Presbyterian distinctives was the commitment to the Westminster Standards and to Calvinism as the system of doctrine taught therein. Another Southern Presbyterian of an earlier age had described this distinctive in this way:

> Perhaps the most prominent characteristic of this Church is jealous loyalty to the Westminster Standards. It holds with unwavering firmness to the undiluted Calvinism of those Standards...This jealous loyalty demands of the minister strict creed subscription. (R. C. Reed, History of the Presbyterian Churches of the World, (Philadelphia:, 1912), p. 286.)

The second question of the ordination vows to which every officer in the PCUS had to subscribe said, "Do you sincerely receive and adopt the Confession of Faith and the Catechisms of this Church as containing the system of doctrine taught in the Holy Scriptures?" (*Book of Church Order*, par 140, 153; in new book 27-6.) The question of what constitutes the "system of doctrine" was raised several times in the PCUS history.

The Assembly of 1898 answered this way, "The words 'system of doctrine' as applied to the whole body of truth contained in the Confession of Faith, being not ambiguous, but sufficiently definite and plain, the Assembly considers it unnecessary, and therefore, declines to give any further definition." (*M1898GAl*, p. 223; *Digest of the Minutes*, 1861-1965, p. 213.)

In 1934, a new request for a definition of this term was requested. The Assembly again declined to give such a definition. It said, "But it cannot determine abstractly, apart from regular judicial process, how the presbytery, under which our Constitution is charged with the duty of ordaining candidates, is to interpret this requirement in the regular discharge of its own functions. To attempt to do so would be in effect to amend the Constitution by extra-constitutional methods." (M1934GA, p. 32; Digest, pp. 213-214.)

The 1939 Assembly did affirm the same five Fundamentals, which the Northern Church had affirmed in 1910 and 1923. While the Northern Church had rejected these fundamentals through the Auburn Affirmation in 1924, it was a full twenty-three years later that the 1947 Southern Church General Assembly clarified the 1939 action, calling it "merely an *in thesi* deliverance, interpreting a part of the content of the ordination vows without any intention of changing the whole substance of them" (M1947GA, p. 45; Digest, p. 214)

In 1972, the Assembly adopted a paper on "Doctrinal Loyalty" in which it says, "In the present situation it is more ambiguous, and whether it can still be useful will depend in part on the degree of theological unanimity now desired by the church." (M1972GA, p. 199.) Here the question raised is the legitimacy of seeking "theological unanimity." In other words, the church no longer held to a serious subscription to the Standards, or the Calvinistic system of doctrine set forth in the Westminster Standards.

The third distinctive of the Southern Presbyterian Church was the doctrine of the "spiritual mission of the Church." Simply stated, this said that the church as a church has just one task handed to her, namely, the task set forth in the Great Commission. She is not to become involved in political or social issues. Individual Christians may and should be so involved. They are to be instructed in everything that God's word teaches, in order to know how to behave in the various spheres of life. Thus, it is proper for individual Christians to be involved in political and social issues, but these are not functions of the church.

World War I brought pressure on the church to endorse a war to end all wars. Following the war, a reaction set in to the effect that the church must never again endorse war, and a spirit of pacifism pervaded much of the church. The question of social injustice also bothered many, and the church was called upon to stand for justice for all. This, of course, is true, but the third distinctive proscribes that it is not the task of the church as a church to become involved in social action. With the Depression and the issue of poverty across the nation, great pressure was placed on the church to become directly involved. The result was the establishment of committees on moral and social welfare.

The Synod of Virginia established such a committee in 1933. Other courts of the church followed suit. In 1934, the General Assembly established a Committee on Moral and Social Welfare. In 1945, after WWII, the Committee was changed to the Council on Christian Relations, and allowed to speak directly to the church, without first getting permission of the Assembly. In 1966, this Council had become a Division of Church and Society within the Board of Christian Education. The Assembly in that year adopted a paper entitled, "Theological Basis for Christian Social Action," claiming that it is the responsibility of individuals *and the church* (emphasis added) to involve themselves in political, social, economic, and cultural life of the world. From this survey, it is obvious that the Southern Church moved from her original distinctive of the spiritual mission of the church.

The emphasis on biblical polity was also one of the distinctive positions of the Southern Presbyterian Church, the fourth we will look at. By the 1940s, the Southern Church had largely forgotten its heritage in the area of polity. Thornwell had argued against semi-autonomous boards, and urged the use of committees to assist the various courts in carrying out the Great Commission. Thus, the church adopted the use of committees over which the Assembly kept close scrutiny. With a new generation of men taught by the liberals in the seminary faculties, the Assembly in 1947 changed the names of the executive committees to boards. This was accomplished with hardly a protest. Thompson says, "A new generation had arisen to whom the disputes of yesterday were unknown." No doubt, this move was also to conform the Southern structure to that of the Northern Church, with organic union in view.

A presbytery could and did control who a congregation could call as minister, but a major stroke against the fourth distinctive was the establishment of a mandatory commission on the minister and his work at the presbytery level. The search committee of the congregation had to present the names of all the ministers being considered. Many commissions abused their authority by assuming the right to approve or disapprove all of these candidates. This often gave to a small group in the presbytery the right of determining whom the congregations could call. In effect, this was the abandonment of the Presbyterian principle that each congregation has the right of election of their officers, including their ministers.

As we review the history of American Presbyterianism, it must be admitted that the mainline denominations, both North and South had a glorious early heritage, a heritage that has been almost totally squandered by the church.

The Southern Church saw herself as holding the Old School position, which gave rise to the Southern Presbyterian distinctives. With the passing of the first generation of leaders, the Southern Church was unable to replace them with men of equal soundness and stature. The result is that the Southern Church lasted as a sound denomination for seventy or eighty years, and then was taken over by the liberals in the church. This was done very largely through the capturing of the educational agencies of the church, the seminaries, the colleges, the publications and literature.

## Chapter Sixteen
## The Founding of the PCA

This account is that of personal word from Dr. Charles Dunahoo and is written in the first person.

I have committed my life to the PCA not because it is a perfect church, but because I believe that the PCA is a true church and a movement of God—a result of His mighty acts. The PCA has been an excitingly predictable, and unpredictable, church during these thirty-two years. For about three years in the 80s we were the fastest growing denomination in America and are still among the top. David Shiflett in his new book, *Exodus, Why Americans are Fleeing Liberal Churches for Conservative Christianity*, states that the PCA has grown by 42.4% during the past ten years. Though we started with churches mainly in the Southeast our intent and design was to be a national church reflected in our first choice of names, The National Presbyterian Church. We quickly put teeth in that commitment as churches began to join us from other parts of the country. Though we did not reach the 2,000 church mark by the year 2,000 as originally projected, we are a church that I believe is making a difference. God has brought some key people, clergy, laity, men and women into our ranks.

Let me state upfront as we talk about the founding of the Presbyterian Church in America in December 1973 that the original 249 churches and 40,000 members came from the Presbyterian Church of United States (PCUS or the Southern Presbyterian Church). We strongly insisted that we were the continuing Southern Presbyterian Church. Those of us in that number felt that the mainline mother denomination over a period of years had so weakened its commitment to the

Scriptures and the Westminster Standards that we could no longer be a part of that denomination.

As a young pastor not long out of seminary, I was one of the six representatives from my presbytery in Alabama at the 1969 PCUS Assembly that met in Mobile, AL. That Assembly concluded there was no contradiction between organic evolution and the Bible. A decision was also made to memorialize Dr. Martin Luther King, civil rights leader who openly questioned the basic fundamentals of the gospel. Though I have in my scrapbook, articles from many newspapers sent to me from around the country thanking me and quoting things that I said in both debates, I experienced less than a favorable reception of my speeches on the floor debating those issues. I remember coming back to Montgomery, AL saying that I felt more and more uncomfortable in a church that I had joined as a young Christian because of the doctrinal commitment to the Westminster Standards and the commitment to the Scriptures. While I grieved somewhat over thoughts of leaving the church where I felt I had found a home, my grief was more because I was so disappointed in that church. I had already struggled with both Liberalism and Neo-orthodox theology while in seminary. I felt I had to stand for the truth and say to a generation of my young peers that truth is real, it is total, and we cannot turn from it without grave consequences. It was at that point that I really became involved in a movement that finally led to the formation of the PCA. I will say more about this later.

The formation of the Presbyterian Church in America did not happen overnight. It was a work in process. I must confess at times I asked, "Will anything good come from this or should I simply leave the Southern Church and join another biblically Reformed church?" At one point, I even laid the groundwork to do that when all of a sudden it appeared that something was on the horizon that might make a difference. Hence, several men whom I had grown to love, appreciate and respect in my denomination, as well as men in the Orthodox Presbyterian Church and the Reformed Presbyterian Church Evangelical Synod counseled me not to leave but to try to have some input in the continuing church movement. I prayed long and hard, listened to my counselors, and decided to do just that, and God honored that prayer in ways that I had not anticipated. (He's good at that).

With that brief anecdotal introductory testimony, I want to highlight some of the major dates and events that led to the formation of the PCA and some things that have happened since that time. In the previous chapter, Dr. Smith pointed out two main things. First, a few of the primary distinctives of the Presbyterian Church in the United States, the Southern Church, in relation to its organization, and second, the departures from those distinctives.

Let me say that in one sense, the beginnings of the PCA can be dated back to the early 1940s. In the sense that there were those such as Dr. John R. Richardson, Dr Nelson Bell, and Rev. Henry Dendy, and a bit later, G. Aiken Taylor, who expressed the concern regarding the turn of direction in the Southern Presbyterian Church by establishing a publication, *The Southern Presbyterian Journal*, later called the *Presbyterian Journal*. The purpose of that publication was to alert the church to the new winds blowing in the church. They also wanted to have a vehicle to call the church back to a strong stance for the Scriptures and the historic Reformed faith. Thirty years after their 1942 beginning, that publication and its leaders became one of the four groups that came together to call for the organization of a Continuing Presbyterian Church. For years, they had sponsored the annual Journal Day meetings in the Weaverville/Asheville area to rally those committed to the church and its biblically Reformed and historic faith.

As things progressed over the next fifteen to sixteen years, the church continued to move further and further from its historical foundings; hence another organization, Presbyterian Evangelistic Fellowship was formed, primarily under the leadership of William (Bill) Hill, a pastor in Hopewell, Virginia and later Ben Wilkinson, a pastor in Mississippi. Their emphasis was to seek to revive the church by strong biblical gospel preaching. They developed a group of men who moved about the church conducting evangelistic meetings and Bible studies. PEF became the second of the group of four that finally called for the organizing of a continuing Presbyterian church—and is the one organization that continues to function yet today. (You may learn more about them at *www.pefministry.org*.)

As the PCUS continued to move away from its original doctrine and polity, a group of laymen under the leadership of Kenneth Keyes (a ruling elder from Miami, FL) and others (including ruling elder Jack Williamson of Greenville, AL, the first Moderator of the PCA) formed another organization known as Concerned Presbyterians in 1964. The Concerned Presbyterians attempted to organize, inform and mobilize the ruling elders in each presbytery to come forward and seek to reclaim the church to its foundation. They organized in the various presbyteries with an emphasis on education, knowing what was happening in the denomination, becoming more involved in the courts of the church, and organizing prayer movements in each presbytery. Not only would a presbytery group of Concerned Presbyterians meet before each presbytery meeting to discuss and prepare for issues that were anticipated on the agenda, the prayer group would intercede on behalf of the purity of the church.

Men's Prayer Fellowship was formed as part of that group. I was asked to lead the prayer group in East Alabama presbytery where I pastored a church in Montgomery. That was the third group that came together in the late 60s and early 70s to help form the PCA. There were hopes and desires that God might enable the PCUS to return to its original mission and purpose.

Without being too anecdotal at this point, I will simply say that in 1968, in Atlanta, GA, a group of ministers met to discuss the current church situation. Growing out of that meeting, a declaration was written and signed by more than 500 ministers calling the church to return to its original commitment. This was done under the leadership of men like Robert Strong (then pastor of the Trinity Presbyterian Church in Montgomery, AL), Donald Patterson (of McIlwain Presbyterian Church in Pensacola, FL and later of First Presbyterian Church in Jackson, MS) and James Baird (of Gadsden, AL and later of Macon, GA). An executive committee of twelve of those 500 was formed. I was asked to serve on that executive committee to represent the younger members of the church. It was given the name Presbyterian Churchmen United and it became the fourth and final group that came together actually to form the PCA.

During those years, attempts were made to peacefully separate from the mainline church. It was apparent that the church would not return to its founding principles. So, it finally looked as though a possibility was looming on the horizon. At that time, during the late 60s and early 70s, attempts were being made to reunite the Northern and Southern Presbyterian Churches. The Northern Church in 1967 had adopted a *Book of Confessions* in which several choices, including the Neo-orthodox Barmen Declaration was included. This meant that if the Southern and Northern Churches would reunite, that would give the continuing church movement the opportunity it had longed for, to leave peacefully with their properties.

Of our number, Jack Williamson was elected to serve on the 24-man committee seeking to develop that union. This committee comprised recommendations from all four of the primary organizations leading the way—Presbyterian Journal, PEF, Concerned Presbyterians and PCU. The agreement was that if the conservatives would support the merger and vote in favor, they would be allowed to use the escape clause, to leave peacefully, and to hold on to the church properties. Actually, this committee made an announcement before a packed house at Weaverville High School in August of 1972 that the formation of a new denomination was not far away.

I confess I was a minority voice who objected to that procedure of allowing the merger to proceed so we could use the escape clause. How could I vote for something I did not think was right in order to get what I thought was right? That was my dilemma; however, that soon became a non-issue because at the last minute, from a February 1973 meeting in New Orleans, we received word from Williamson that the escape clause had been removed from the merger plans. Many in our group felt betrayed and decided we could delay no longer. Therefore, at that February meeting of the 24-man committee we finally took the bold step and called for convocation of sessions.

Thirty churches in the Southern Church initiated this original call for convocation of sessions. My church in the Atlanta area was one of the thirty. We met at the Westminster Presbyterian Church in Atlanta. The meeting was held in May of that year, 1973. A call went forth from that convocation to establish a continuing Presbyterian church faithful to Scriptures, the Reformed faith, and the Great Commission. A few present at that convocation resisted the formation of a new denomination, but the large majority was committed to continuing a Presbyterian church in the historical tradition of the early Southern Church.

An organizing committee of forty and an executive committee were elected to plan a convention to be held in Asheville, NC in August of 1973. I was on both the committee of forty and the executive committee. I had the privilege of helping plan the next major events. The advisory convention was to be held in August of 1973.

Meeting at the Grove Park Inn in Asheville, NC, in August of 1973, the Advisory Convention gathered. That meeting opened with worship led by Cecil Williamson, a pastor in Selma, AL and the word was preached by Robert Ostenson, pastor of a church in Coral Gables, FL. The convention began to put into place the mechanics of forming a continuing Presbyterian church in the fashion described above. Provisional committees were established and assignments were made to prepare for convening a date in December of 1973, which would officially mark the beginning of a newly formed denomination. Even though the numbers were small in comparison with those of the mainline church, the convention received a large amount of publicity. Some of us had already withdrawn and formed provisional presbyteries. Some of us had already been defrocked because of such action. Others awaited possible discipline and the loss of church property.

The organizing committee attempted to follow the same pattern used by the old Southern Presbyterian denomination at its formation in 1861. Hence, the Advisory Convention set the structures and framework whereby the new denomination could be established and would hopefully operate on an ongoing basis. For example, I was asked to chair the committee on constitutional documents. One part of the committee led by Dr. Morton Smith focused to the adoption of the Westminster Standards, and the other part of us, with me serving as chairman, concentrated on the *Book of Church Order (BCO)*, which finally involved a three-year process of presenting and adopting by the first three Assemblies. After the vote to adopt the recommended editions of the doctrinal standards contained in the Westminster Confession of Faith, and Larger and Shorter Catechisms, that committee merged with those of us working with the *Book of Church Order* and we became the Constitutional Documents Committee. Morton Smith and I worked side by side. We also had excellent input from other committee members such as Don Patterson, Frank Barker and John Barnes.

At the Asheville Advisory Convention, we had invited representatives from the Orthodox Presbyterian Church and the Reformed Presbyterian Church to meet with us in order to draw from their wisdom and expertise. Representatives from other organizations were there as well, such as Westminster Presbyterian Church in Perth, Australia, Presbyterian Church of Zaire, and a representative from the Reformed Ecumenical Synod.

That convention was a lively, exciting and energetic convention. The spiritual tone, with excitement, permeated the Grove Park Inn. There were debates over this and that issue. At least one major newspaper picked up on some of the debates especially when one zealous participant declared to poke anyone in the nose who said he had to support all the work of the church, one of the founding principles of the new church. The headlines read something to the effect of "Small

Conservative Group Already Fighting Amongst Themselves."
However, the group went forward. Many were saying the
group would not hold together as it would split and splinter
early on. By the grace of God and the desire of the participants
to be a part of a biblical Reformed church, with doctrinal
integrity, evangelistic fervor and practical spirituality, the call of
the organization was set in place. We also believe that God
used the influence of Dr. Francis Schaeffer to remind us that
we were the church before the watching world and therefore
we attempted to avoid some of the divisions experienced by
earlier groups.

Working under the provisional Christian Education and
Publications Committee (CE&P), a group of women met as the
Women in the Church. Mrs. Gordon Reed (Miriam) served as
chair. They were asked to organize and develop a suggested
constitution for local churches and presbyteries to use in the
women's ministries. WIC was to be a subcommittee for advice
and research working under the supervision and authority of
CE&P, as well as partnering with them in developing many
different ministries and curricula.

The final report of the Advisory Convention contained this
statement:

> In the name of our Lord Jesus Christ we call to
> convene in holy assembly the duly elected
> representatives of sessions and ministers who subscribe
> to the text and commitment of the Reaffirmations
> of 1973 and who meet such other credential
> requirements as established by the Convention.

> This Assembly is hereby called to convene at
> Briarwood Presbyterian Church, Birmingham, AL on
> December 4, 1973 at 7 p.m.

The purpose of this Assembly shall be:

a.  To worship Almighty God in the name of the Father, the Son, and the Holy Spirit.

b.  To petition God the Father that, by His Spirit, this people be constituted under His Son as a reborn Presbyterian Church and that their representatives there assembled be constituted the 1st General Assembly of this reborn church.

c.  To act upon all advice and recommendations laid before them by this Convention.

d.  To conclude such other matters as the Assembly it may deem meet and proper in these premises.

The December 4-7, 1973 dates were chosen for the 1st General Assembly. It was partly acknowledgment of our great heritage that the same date (December 4) of the convening of the initial General Assembly of the Southern Presbyterian Church in 1861 was chosen. Plans were made to convene in Birmingham, Alabama at Briarwood Presbyterian Church. One of the first items of business was to elect a Moderator and a Stated Clerk. W. Jack Williamson was elected Moderator and Morton Smith, Stated Clerk. As stated above, Williamson was a lawyer from Greenville, AL and a key player in the Concerned Presbyterians, the Presbyterian Journal, and with the steering committees and the organizing committee. Morton Smith, a founding professor of theology at Reformed Theological Seminary was elected as the first Stated Clerk. Initially, it was a part-time job. Morton Smith served the church in that capacity for nearly twenty years. In the fall of 1977, he was elected to that position full-time and left the seminary in order to serve.

At the 1$^{st}$ Assembly, the organizational structure was officially put into place. Having adopted the founding principles set forth in Part One of the *BCO*, and having adopted the theology of the church, the structure to reflect those was approved. The Assembly established the following three documents or sources of its operational procedures: *Robert's Rules of Order*, the *Book of Church Order* and the *Rules of Assembly Operations*. Those three have guided the church for its thirty-three years.

When the PCA, first called the National Presbyterian Church, was organized, a typical and expected thing occurred. It tended to organize in somewhat of a reactionary manner to things that were judged not to be right in the mother denomination, the PCUS. As the youngest participant on the executive committee of committee of forty, I frequently urged the others not to throw out the baby with the bath water by assuming all the organizational principles and practices of the mother church were at fault. However, growing out of that context, there was such a longtime feeling of distrust and betrayal, along with a lack of biblical and theological integrity within the PCUS, that the National Presbyterian Church came into existence in a very definite but disjointed fashion. This was demonstrated by the vote to place the four permanent committees in separate locations. Even though there were some practical reasons for such an action that was not the main reason for such action. The original locations were chosen because of the location of the first coordinators who were chosen to lead those committees.

The work of the church was defined in the *BCO* as "one work," expressed through its committees and agencies. It's theology of understanding and implementing the Great Commission led the PCA to establish three ministry (or program) committees, Mission to the World, Mission to the United States, and Christian Education and Publications. However, many saw the new church's mission in less than a holistic light. Some of that was the result of not being taught the biblical nature of the church and its theology, and some was simply a reaction of not being able to support certain ministries in the mainline church because of liberal philosophy. Therefore, churches were to have the freedom to support parts of the church's mission and not the whole, if they so chose. Churches were not required nor obligated to support the work of the committees. This in effect meant that the committees were responsible to raise their own funds from the beginning. As a member of the first Administration Committee, we attempted to balance the parts with the whole, but only to finally realize that the committees' budgets tended to be looked on as "hunting licenses."

As one of the authors of the church's organizing principles in the *BCO*, I can affirm that our attempt was to create a theologically ecclesial unity. The work of the church was defined as "one work." However, connection between the committees was arbitrary. There was no Assembly-given structural mandate set in place to facilitate a close working together. As a matter of fact, when the recommendation to place the committees together in one city was made, one well-known commissioner stated in the debate that, "If we put them together, they might start working together."

There are a number of important facts that are worth highlighting, and in fact, worth remembering about the formation of the PCA.

First, the PCA was not formed in a vacuum, i.e., starting from zero. There were 249 churches, some of considerable size. There were 40,000 initial members.

Second, when the church organized it adopted the name the National Presbyterian Church because though it originated in the southeast, our desire was to be a truly national church. There was a local congregation in Washington, D.C. known as The National Presbyterian Church, however, that objected to our choosing that name. Though we knew we could win a lawsuit because we were a denomination, not a local church, we decided at the 2nd General Assembly to change the name to the Presbyterian Church in America (PCA) which has been our title since 1974.

Third, the PCA has always had a strong emphasis on world missions. It took over a group, established by Presbyterian Evangelistic Fellowship, known as ECOE (Executive Committee for Overseas Evangelism) with a $100,000 budget and several missionaries already in place. Even today, the largest portion of the PCA's benevolences goes to support missionaries in forty-seven countries. While it has been exciting to say that we have the largest Presbyterian mission agency, this has created difficulty for the other committees and agencies in raising support.

Growing out of a contentious debate for several years, brought to an overwhelmingly approved compromise during the 3rd General Assembly, Mission to the World was authorized to cooperate through partnership agreements with parachurch agencies working in various parts of the world, subject to approval of those agreements by vote of the General Assembly. This was one of the issues that brought about the 1937 split in the PCofA. Thus, the PCA wisely found a middle ground and many believe this has enabled MTW to grow as fast and as large as it has.

Fourth, the PCA was established to be a grassroots church with representation from all levels of the church. Its desire has been not to be dominated by the clergy; hence the commitment to maintain an open General Assembly. This has not developed in the fashion hoped for. While the PCA adopted a somewhat innovative definition of parity between ruling and teaching elders, the General Assembly representation is always more than two-to-one teaching elders in contrast to ruling elders. An attempt to achieve a balance continues to be a challenge for the PCA. We continue to try to encourage the participation of ruling elders at the annual PCA General Assembly, at local presbytery meeting, and in churches.

Fifth, is the principle built into the formation of the PCA that each congregation clearly and without challenge, owns its own property and neither the presbytery nor the Assembly has any claim on it except at the vote of a particular congregation. This means that a local church can withdraw from the denomination at its pleasure with its properties.

Sixth, having no Sunday school curriculum of its own, the Christian Education and Publications Committee, assigned that task, recommended the curriculum of the Orthodox Presbyterian Church known as Great Commission Publications. Two years later, with approval of both the OPC and the PCA through their Christian education committees, a full partnership and ownership of GCP was established. We celebrated that thirty-year partnership at the 2005 Assembly. It has been a good and profitable ministry and has provided local churches with good, solidly biblical and Reformed Sunday school curriculum consistent with the philosophy of making kingdom disciples who understand the Scriptures from a historical redemptive perspective.

Seventh, having no seminary of its own in the beginning, the Christian Education and Publications Committee did two things First, they recommended that Westminster, Covenant, and Reformed Theological Seminaries be used to train future PCA pastors. Second, they recommended that an alternative track training program also be developed and approved, under the supervision of CE&P, which would train men for the gospel ministry in several different ways (other than through seminary education), depending on the presbytery's choices.

The PCA is a church with a unique commitment to Jesus Christ, his word, and the Reformed faith but not in some narrow isolationist's sense where we demonstrate only a fortress mentality and talk only to ourselves. We desire to see people converted to Christ and discipled in the faith; to see churches built solidly upon his word, and nations impacted by our missionary effort. We are also a church that from day one has not only committed itself to being Reformed in doctrine but Calvinistic in our worldview.

I will not repeat Dr. Smith's explanation of the Southern Presbyterian Church's distinctives from the previous chapter but only to say, they were the same for the PCA and the RPCES. The Declaration to All Churches, adopted by the 1st PCA General Assembly, reflected those distinctives and issued an invitation to all who shared our commitment to join with us.

In the next chapter we will follow the history of how that commitment finally worked itself out with the Joining and Receiving of the RPCES.

## Chapter Seventeen
## "Joining and Receiving" – The Roots
## Come Back Together

A s was pointed out in the previous chapter, the Presbyterian Church in America never viewed itself as simply a southern, regional church— although that is certainly where it began. In fact, at the very first General Assembly in 1973 in Birmingham, a resolution was approved by vote of the Assembly, which reads in part:

1. That the Interchurch Relations Committee be authorized and hereby directed to place suitable notices in appropriate religious publications throughout the United States extending the right hand of fellowship to all Christians of the Presbyterian and Reformed tradition who believe in the Scriptures of the Old and New Testaments as the Word of God written, and

2. That the Interchurch Relations Committee be specifically authorized to correspond with the similar committees of the Orthodox Presbyterian Church, the Reformed Presbyterian Church, Evangelical Synod, and the Reformed Presbyterian Church of North America (ed; Covenanter Synod), and

3. That any correspondence resulting from these contacts be explored as possibilities for broadening and strengthening the spirit of love and understanding between Christians in the United States who believe the Bible as the Word of God written, the Reformed Faith, and the Presbyterian order.

It is clear from these words that the PCA wanted, as a minimum, to have fraternal relations with like-minded groups— and some even interpreted those words as a desire to seek organic union. At the next two assemblies, the PCA was authorized to join a functional organization known as the North American Presbyterian and Reformed Council (NAPARC) and spelled out that this membership would be limited only to:

1. Exchange of fraternal delegates at major assemblies

2. Occasional pulpit fellowship

3. Intercommunion (i.e. fellowship at the Table of the Lord)

4. Joint action in areas of common responsibility

5. Communication on major issues of joint concern

6. The exercise of mutual concern and admonition with a view to promoting the fundamentals of Christian unity.

As you can see, there is no language whatsoever that would point to or foresee any organic union coming through this group. At the time of its organization, NAPARC included the PCA, the CRC, the OPC, the RPCES, and the RPCNA.

By the time of the 4th General Assembly (1976) held in Greenville, South Carolina, the Interchurch Relations Committee (IRC) began slowly to move forward the idea of organic union in the future. One of their recommendations adopted that year reads as follows:

That this General Assembly acknowledge with gratitude and Christian love the communication of the

General Synod of the RPCES of May, 1976, regarding our common ecumenical concerns, also the action of the General Assembly of the OPC, May, 1976 in instructing its Committee on Ecumenicity and Interchurch Relations to study a similar communication. In response this General Assembly requests its own Committee on Interchurch Relations, together with the Moderator, Past-Moderators, and the Clerk of the GA as Ex-officio members to consider carefully the matters suggested by the RP communication, and, furthermore, to endeavor to fashion a long range policy of mutual concern, activities, and the pursuance of unity with these denominations, reporting to the next General Assembly. We remind sister churches that we are still an infant denomination and that obligations we feel for the firm establishment of our church and of our congregations require that we avoid any appearance of haste in these matters. At the same time, we take this initial step so as to support those biblical principles which place us under the divine tension of unity in the body of Christ visible, wherever and however this may be encouraged or engaged without compromise of our standards or of our primary responsibilities to our members churches.

Even this very tentative—some would say watered down—language was not approved by everyone present at that Assembly, although it was passed by a clear majority.

The next year (1977) at Smyrna, Georgia, the Interchurch Relations Committee (ICR) took one more baby step forward with the adoption of this motion:

The Assembly authorizes the Committee on ICR to continue their present discussions with other Reformed bodies including discussion of possible union with the

RPCES and OPC, but that any proposal of official action on union will be withheld until the paper on the biblical basis of ecclesiastical union and fraternal relations is received by the General Assembly.

The 6th General Assembly of the PCA was purposely held in Grand Rapids, Michigan at the same time that several sister denominations were holding their annual meetings—including the Christian Reformed Church (the meetings were held at Calvin College and Calvin Seminary), the OPC and the RPCES. When the issue of merger discussions came to the floor, the Interchurch Relations Committee (IRC) was divided—bringing a strongly worded minority report asking that the PCA not enter into any talks that might result in merger or organic union. However, the majority report of the committee was adopted as follows:

> Since the report (on Biblical Basis for Church Union) demonstrates that church union of brethren who hold the Reformed Faith in common is biblical, we recommend that the General Assembly authorize the Interchurch Relations Committee to discuss the factors involved with and the possibility of working toward a merger of the PCA with the OPC and the RPCES, with the understanding that the discussions do not imply commitment to ultimate merger.

In typical PCA fashion, not only were a number of "nay's" voiced when the vote was taken (although the "ayes" had it), a number of men felt conscience bound to have their negative votes recorded in the record. Clearly, there was a strong resistance to moving ahead.

The 7th General Assembly was held in Charlotte, North Carolina on June 18-22, 1979. The IRC met twice during the year, the second time in St. Louis in February where they met with their OPC and RPCES counterparts. The result of the joint meeting was the following recommendation:

> It is the opinion of the Joint Committees of the Fraternal Relations Committees of the OPC, the PCA, and the RPCES that as Presbyterian Churches, committed to a common faith as set forth in the Westminster Standards, and to the Presbyterian form of government, and to a common testimony to the purity of the Church, we have a basis for merger of the three Churches. We, therefore, recommend to the respective Committees that they each recommend to their Churches the continuation of consultations with a plan of merger in view." *(Minutes of the 7GA, p178, IRC Report)*

When the report of the Committee of Commissioners (the Assembly's review committee of the IRC) came to the floor on Tuesday afternoon, they brought it in two parts. The first was to discuss the merits of and then decide whether a 3/4 (supermajority) vote should be required. The debate on that part was both strong and divided. Less than a sixty percent majority approved the requirement of a 3/4 vote (285-204) on the second recommendations forthcoming.

When the actual recommendation to continue the consultations towards a plan of merger was presented, the debate was again sharply divided and strong. There were some who were opposed to the idea of including the OPC in consultations rather than the concept in general, and there were others who just plain did not want to have merger discussions with anyone. Several of the speeches emphasized that the PCA was still too young and searching for her own identity.

The final vote was 353 for, 208 against, a sixty-two percent majority, thus failing the 3/4 vote requirement set earlier, and even failing the normal 2/3 requirement. (*Minutes of 7GA*, p. 95, Section 7-34.) It was clear that the Assembly was not ready to move towards a merger.

However, there were some commissioners who were ready! That afternoon, three commissioners who had come from RPCES roots and who had been classmates at Covenant Seminary in the early 70s, developed a motion to try to keep some momentum moving forward. The three men included your author, along with TE Fred Marsh (then a pastor in the Chattanooga area) and TE Rick Tyson (then a pastor in Ballston Spa, New York). We drafted the following motion:

Since Item 5b of the Report of the Committee of Commissioners received a majority vote, but less than 3/4, the following action is recommended:

1. That an *Ad Interim* Committee be appointed by the General Assembly to meet with representatives of the RPCES, the OPC and the RPCNA with instructions not to develop any plan of union, but merely to determine possible areas of agreement, difference and difficulty that might exist between the three denominations

2. That the committee be appointed by the General Assembly of three ruling elders and three teaching elders, members to be nominated by the Committee on Nominations

3. That this Committee be funded in the same manner as the Committee on Interchurch Relations, and

4. That this Committee report its findings to the 1980 General Assembly through the Committee of Commissioners on Interchurch Relations.

As drafters who had voted on the losing side, we had to ask someone who had voted on the prevailing side to ask for Reconsideration in order to get the motion on the floor. The request was made of TE Gordon Reed. Gordon was a member of the IRC. He had spoken against adopting the motion on the floor and clearly was on the prevailing side.

Gordon agreed to make the motion. On Thursday he went to the floor and asked to make a motion to amend the ICR report and was given permission by a 2/3 vote. The item was then docketed for immediately after lunch. After lunch Gordon made the motion to appoint the Ad-Interim Committee and with a minimal amount of debate it passed by an overwhelming majority, 418-82. (*Minutes of 7GA*, p. 134, Section 7-73.) This was a clear sign the Assembly wanted to say something to the OPC and RPCES to avoid the adverse affect if the matter ended simply with the defeat of a supermajority vote.

The men then elected to serve on this *Ad Interim* Committee (after being nominated by the Nominating Committee) were TE Carl Bogue, Ascension Presbytery; RE Rob Cannada, Sr., Mississippi Valley Presbytery; RE Ed Robeson, Calvary Presbytery; TE Paul Settle, Calvary Presbytery; TE William J. Stanway, Grace Presbytery; and RE Jack Williamson, Evangel Presbytery. TE Settle was appointed to act as Convener and he was subsequently elected as Chairman at the first meeting.

This *Ad Interim* Committee met on September 14, 1979 and had invited representatives of the Fraternal Relations Committees of the RPCES, RPCNA and OPC to meet with them. After a series of joint discussions, the PCA *Ad Interim*

Committee met and unanimously included the following notation as part of their report:

> The question was raised in the joint meeting of the various denominational representatives as to whether or not the PCA would be receptive to the idea of inviting the RPCES, for example, to come into the PCA under terms of the PCA *Book of Church Order* without the necessity of prolonged negotiations to develop a plan for denominational merger (See *BCO* 15-6). There was discussion of the organizational structure of the PCA and the provision for receiving congregations from another denomination on a congregation-by-congregation basis. So far as any proposal for action was concerned, the PCA *Ad Interim* Committee recognized that its function was strictly a fact finding function and it could go no further than that. Such a proposal might be initiated by presbytery overtures or through recommendation of the Sub-committee on Interchurch Relations of the Committee on Administration." *(Minutes 8GA, p. 239, Committee report).*

There really is no other way to evaluate this recommendation. This was the birth of the concept that quickly became known as Joining and Receiving. It is my understanding that the idea was first surfaced by one of the RPCES representatives, Don MacNair, then serving as director of the RPCES Church Planting arm.

This should come as no surprise when you consider the position the EPC took in their merger talks with the RPC, General Synod. In many respects, the EPC did an "almost" Joining and Receiving to bring about that merger.

The *Ad Interim* Committee's recommendation came to the floor of the 8th General Assembly in Savannah on Tuesday June 17, 1980. The Committee on Interchurch Relations had proposed the adoption of a letter to be sent to the RPCES, the RPCNA, and the OPC asking them to pursue Joining and Receiving with us. This was a very positive, major step they were recommending. The Committee of Commissioners had drafted a more moderate motion that sought to state the principles without making an overt "invitation." Their motion was a brief and concise one as follows:

That the 8th General Assembly of the PCA reaffirm at this time that portion of its original letter from our 1st General Assembly to all Churches, which reads: "As this new member of the family of Churches of the Lord Jesus Christ comes into being, we necessarily profess the biblical doctrine of the unity of all who are in Christ...We greet all believers in an affirmation of the bond of Christian brotherhood. We invite into ecclesiastical fellowship all who maintain our principles of faith and order.

Committees of Commissioners were required to express a written reason for why they proposed responses, and their reasons were given as follows:

The Sub-Committee on Interchurch Relations has responded to new channels of discussion with other Churches of like confessional base for which we are grateful. However, the Committee of Commissioners feels that the substance of the letter proposed in the Sub-Committee Recommendation Number 4 may have been inappropriate in view of the actions of the 7th General Assembly.

The Committee of Commissioners version of any recommendation is presented first to the General Assembly. Immediately after their motion was made, there was a substitute motion to adopt the more aggressive language of the Permanent Sub-Committee which read:

To: RPCES, RPCNA, and OPC

Subject: An invitation to effect one Church.

Brethren: Greetings in the Names of the Lord Jesus Christ, the King and Head of the Church.

Whereas, we hold to and desire to promote a common testimony to the inerrancy of Scripture, the system of doctrine contained in the Westminster Confession of Faith and Catechisms, and the doctrine of the purity of the visible Church; and

Whereas, we feel constrained by our commitments to seek a more perfect unity among us as members of Christ's body;

Now therefore, the General Assembly of the Presbyterian Church in America in the bonds of our Lord Jesus Christ, invites you to come with us for the purpose of effecting and perfecting one Church among us. We propose, as the basis for this association, the above named principles, together with the Book of Church Order of the Presbyterian Church in America.

Because the complexity of the issues before the General Assembly—there had been four overtures from presbyteries with varying languages, there was a recommendation from the Permanent Sub-Committee, and a different recommendation from the Committee of Commissioners, it was decided to go into a Committee of the Whole in closed session (meaning visitors from other denominations would not be present). The Moderator asked TE James Moore—at that time pastor of the Eastland Church in Memphis and a skilled parliamentarian—to assume the chair.

The Assembly stayed in Committee of the Whole until 11:30 p.m. During that time, we took a "straw vote" and determined that the best course of action was to issue a simple invitation to the RPCES and OPC to "consider matters necessary to effect church union with the PCA." With that work taking us as late as any Assembly had worked until then (the one in Baton Rouge finally set the record) the Assembly recessed to get some sleep.

On Wednesday morning, the action on the matter came to the floor shortly after lunch. The Judicial Business Sub-Committee brought their report, which affirmed that a 3/4 vote of the presbyteries would be required to ratify something like Joining and Receiving and to advise that a phrase in the motion ("the doctrine of the purity of the visible Church") was appropriate for use in the motion.

All was now in place for the continuation of the question. The first action was to actually vote to call all excused committees and commissions back to the floor for the matter before it. There always seemed to be groups required to be off the floor, especially judicial commissions which had to meet during the business time of the Assembly back in those days.

The next action was to adopt a special rule to apply to the discussions on the Interchurch Relations report, increasing the time for each main motion to ten minutes and allowing each individual to speak three minutes.

231

After a break for worship and lunch, the house was full—since the order for all committees and commissions to return was still in force. On the floor was a substitute motion from the previous night with a shortened form of the "letter" which had been proposed by the Permanent Sub-Committee on Interchurch Relations.

Although the straw vote taken the previous night in Closed Session indicated the Assembly desired to do something different, this piece of business was on the floor and had to be dealt with first. In the wisdom of God that sometimes prevails in the light of day after a long, hard night, the straw vote was quickly forgotten and the Assembly debated and finally voted on the letter. This version was approved by a counted vote of 423 affirmative and 124 negative.

Recognizing the importance of the advice received that morning from the Judicial Business Sub-Committee, the Assembly voted to amend the letter by adding additional language. The final form of final paragraph of the letter, including the language recommended by the Judicial Business Sub-Committee was as follows:

> It is to be understood that this invitation is an action of the $8^{th}$ General Assembly, and to receive any denomination which responds to this invitation it should be stated that for the PCA to consummate any such union it would have to go through the constitutional process of approval by subsequent General Assemblies and three-fourths of our presbyteries. In this constitutional process each denomination much be dealt with separately.

The Assembly quickly adopted a motion to make copies of this recommendation, along with the vote tabulation, for commissioners to take home with them. Clearly, this was one of the most dramatic votes taken in the brief history of the PCA. The denomination had just voted to bring some other historical roots of Presbyterianism to join us in the PCA. But in typical Presbyterian fashion, there were still three years of hoops to jump through.

The report of the Committee of Commissioners on Interchurch Relations at the 9th General Assembly, held in Fort Lauderdale, came to the floor at 7:30 p.m. in the evening. But this year—even though the outcome was final and more positive—it still took until 11:30 p.m!

The special *Ad Interim* Committee (the one appointed at the 7th Assembly) had submitted one of the most extensive reports in the history of the denomination. It takes fifty-eight pages of small print in the *Minutes* to cover all the issues, give summaries of the nature of the denominations, show statistical comparisons, a paper written by Stated Clerk Morton Smith summarizing for all concerned how Presbyterian polity was conducted in the PCA, which was of course somewhat different from the other churches, and on, and on. It was a magnificent report—which when you think about it was worthy of the quality of the committee that had been elected two years previously.

Action was taken first on the RPCES. The RPCES had adopted a motion on how they perceived Joining and Receiving should proceed, and the committee recommended the exact same set of procedures. There were provisions for all General Assembly level personnel being given guaranteed jobs for one year. There were provisions for how presbyteries would be formed (and even a map!) There was a provision for how we would receive the college and seminary operated by the RPCES to become PCA institutions. All the "i's" were dotted and "t's" were crossed. The essential, operative motion was this:

> That the General Assembly take the first formal vote under paragraph 14-6 of the *BCO*: "to receive under its jurisdiction, with the consent of three-fourths of the presbyteries, other ecclesiastical bodies whose organization is conformed to the doctrine and order of this church." Thus all ordained officers in the RPCES will be received into the PCA without examination.

Then the requirements for 3/4 of the presbyteries to approve the invitation was passed and the steps for the RPCES were in process.

Next came the recommendation on the OPC being included in Joining and Receiving. The main motion was identical to the one on the RPCES. Immediately there was a substitute motion introduced asking to defer the invitation to the OPC until such time that "the PCA has determined that the current controversy has been resolved in a manner that is in accord with the teaching of Scripture and the Confession...." The motion was referring to an ongoing controversy at Westminster Seminary concerning the teaching on Justification by one of their faculty members, who was at the time an OPC minister. No charges had been brought in the case but there was a lot of talk.

The vote on the substitute to delay failed by a large majority (192 to 347) and then it was time to vote on the main motion to invite the OPC. The vote of invitation was passed 422 to 187 and the OPC had been invited to Join and Receive with the PCA!

A format was put in place to keep track of how the presbytery votes were going and they were all asked to vote as early in the year as possible so all the parties would know prior to planning for the next General Assembly if the coming together of all three denominations would take place. The Assembly was set to meet in Grand Rapids once again so the denominations could have fellowship with each other while the decisions were being made.

However, when the commissioners arrived in Grand Rapids the next year, everyone knew that only one of the two denominations would be invited to Join and Receive. The votes of the presbyteries of the PCA to invite the RPCES was unanimous: 25-0. However, the vote to invite the OPC failed by one presbytery. Nineteen presbyteries voting yes were required to meet the 3/4 requirement. Only eighteen voted yes. One of the presbyteries voting no failed by only two votes to approve: 50-52. In another the vote was 20 yes, 10 no, 10 abstain, which amounted to a 20-20 tie. So, by the margin of the votes of two elders in one presbytery and one elder in another the invitation to the OPC failed.

On Monday morning, June 14, 1982, ruling elder Ken Ryskamp, the outgoing Moderator of the PCA called the 10th General Assembly to order. The very first piece of business was a recommendation from the Committee of Commissioners on Interchurch Relations asked TE Paul Settle, Chairman of the *Ad Interim* Committee to come to the podium and report. He informed the Assembly that a sufficient number of PCA presbyteries had approved the invitation to the RPCES to Join and Receive. He also reported that at the meeting of the Synod of the RPCES (held the previous Saturday there in Grand Rapids) had taken their final vote, and with an affirmative vote of 322 to 90, had voted to accept the invitation. RPCES delegates, who had been duly certified, were declared members of the General Assembly of the PCA.

This was immediately followed by a worship service celebrating the reception of the RPCES into the PCA, with Francis Schaeffer having been invited to preach a special message entitled "A Day of Sober Rejoicing." (For those interested in reading Dr. Schaeffer's address. you may find it at *www.pcanet.org/history/findingaids/schaeffer/JandR.pdf.*)

One might think that this finished any idea of union with the OPC. But there were many men in the PCA that didn't want to give up that easily. At the 11th General Assembly in Norfolk, the PCA voted by the needed 2/3 margin (barely) 441 to 220 to reissue the invitation to the OPC to Join and Receive. Again, this would require a 3/4 vote of the presbyteries. The OPC committee decided not to take any action until the vote of the PCA presbyteries came in.

At the 12th General Assembly, the vote of the presbyteries was announced. With 29 presbyteries required to approve, 29 voted yes, 7 no, 1 was tied. With no margin to spare, yet with enough, the invitation was approved by the presbyteries. It is worth mentioning that because of Joining and Receiving with the RPCES, there were many more presbyteries and many of them had the strong influence of former RPCES members who obviously were voting "yes."

Knowing that the OPC Committee on Ecumenical Affairs was going to take some time to prepare their denomination for a vote, the PCA voted to meet in Philadelphia in 1986, at the same time the OPC would be holding their 50th Anniversary celebration, obviously anticipating the possibility of that being the year the OPC would come into the PCA.

In 1986, the OPC General Assembly met earlier than the PCA and they voted on whether or not to accept the invitation. After sixty-seven speeches on the floor, the vote taken resulted in 78 yes, 68 no—far short of the 3/4 needed by their rules. The OPC had rejected our invitation!

The Committee of Commissioners on Interchurch Relations brought to the floor of the General Assembly that, in spite of their rejection, the PCA would once again issue the invitation to Join and Receive. That motion was adopted by a voice vote, clearly the will of the body.

However, when we arrived at the 15th General Assembly the next year in Grand Rapids, we were informed that with approval of 27 of the PCA presbyteries necessary to confirm the invitation, only 24 had voted yes. This time it felt final. It was over. For whatever reasons God might have and demonstrated through his guidance and providence during the past eight years, it looked like the OPC would not become part of the PCA.

We may never know the reasons the PCA presbyteries once declined, then agreed, and then on a third trip declined. Historians will study closely those presbyteries that consistently voted no and notice that they were predominately in the deep South. That's just a fact—others will have to attach reasons.

The authors of a book entitled *Fighting the Good Fight*, D. G. Hart, a professor of Church History and John Muether, the OPC historian and seminary librarian in Orlando, offer their opinion:

There are perhaps as many explanations for these actions as there were different reasons for the commissioners' votes. Advocates of the merger efforts of 1975 (with the RPCES), 1981 and 1986 argue that the OPC should unite with bodies that hold the same confessional standards. Refusal to do so is backward, inward, and exclusive—not biblical, charitable, and wise. Opponents were not convinced that these sister institutions affirmed the Westminster Standards in acceptable ways. At the heart of this concern was the question of what it means to be 'Reformed'; e.g., would a Reformed church tolerate Arminian and charismatic office bearers? The heated debates on the floor of the OP general assembly brought to light questions about the theological identities of the denominations involved in discussions. (p. 137)

Whatever position one holds, that the PCA should never have asked others to join them, or that it's a shame the OPC didn't come, one thing is for sure. With the addition of the churches and ministers from the RPCES, not only had some historical roots been merged, but the church would never be the same again.

## Chapter Eighteen
## Identifying the Roots and Call to "Plant Pathologists" for a Diagnosis

In this final chapter, I want to focus on the central issue illustrated by the book title: The Historical <u>Roots</u> of the Presbyterian Church in America. The real purpose of the book was not to examine church history in order to determine what the heritage of the PCA might have been. As wonderful as heritage might be, it is essentially irrelevant to current times.

I am half Lithuanian. That is an unusual and very interesting heritage and, for the most part, totally irrelevant—as is the heritage of most individuals. Our heritage has no effect on who we are today. But there is a difference between one's heritage and one's roots. Let me explain.

My maternal grandfather fought in the army of the last Russian Czar. When I entered the Naval Security Group (the Navy's branch of the National Security Agency), I had to undergo an extremely thorough background investigation in order to grant me a Top Secret Cryptographic Codeword clearance. So I had to have my family back in Detroit go through all their papers to find my grandfather's discharge papers to verify that, back in the decade of the 1910s, he was not fighting on the side of the Bolsheviks. The fear of the people granting the clearance was that had he been an early communist and that could have been a "root" in our family, i.e., something that affected what I might have been at the time.

The same goes for a church. Consider the heritage of the mainline Presbyterian Church today, the Presbyterian Church in the United States of America. They, in fact, share the exact same heritage as those of us in the Presbyterian Church in America, up to the beginning of the 20th Century, at least. But as far as the PCUSA is concerned, all that "stuff" from prior to 1900 is simply heritage. In the current website of the PCUSA, under the section for their history, they say this: *"The Presbyterian church traces its ancestry back primarily to Scotland and England."*

But it is simply ancestry, or heritage, if you will. The doctrines for which many were willing to die, and for which many did die—the doctrines of the pre-Reformers, Luther, Calvin, the Swiss Reformers, Knox, the Covenanters, Cranmer, the British reformers, the Puritans, the "Log Cabin" and Princeton Seminary theology—all of that is simply "ancestry" to the PCUSA. But in the PCA, those are our roots.

The Merriam-Webster online dictionary gives the following definition for a root: *"the usually underground part of a seed plant body that…functions as an organ of absorption, aeration, and food storage or as a means of anchorage and support."* A root, you see, is far more than simply heritage. A root is part of a living organism and is, in fact, a part without which the plant will die. So it is vital to the health of a plant (and therefore, vital to the health of the PCA) to be sure the roots are alive and functioning.

As a Presbyterian, I do not believe it is appropriate for one person alone to determine the health of the roots of a denomination. We glory in our rule by multiple elders; a church cannot exist as a church with just one elder. There must be multiple elders to share in the rule. Thus, I think it wise, in this chapter, for me not to state my opinion as to the health of the roots of the PCA, but rather to seek to put together a list of what those roots are. (This isn't the only list, it's just my list.)

After preparing this list, I will issue a call for multiple elders in the PCA to make their examinations of the health of these roots. The easiest way to develop the list is to go back, chapter by chapter, and pull out those principles that I believe must be recognized as roots. Some of this history I consider simply heritage (and great heritage, at that). For instance, I believe that the principle found in the Church of Scotland in their origin, and a principle that found much favor in the early days of Presbyterian Churches in America—the principle of exclusive psalmody—is heritage, and not a root.

Of course, a few would strongly disagree with that analysis. And they may, in fact, disagree with other points on my list. There may be something they feel I left off, or something that should not be on the list. Again, even in this effort, it will take the work of multiple elders to formalize the list of those things that we should consider roots. But we've got to start somewhere and it's my book, so I will step forward and present the first list.

From Chapter One, in which we discussed the history of the Church *before* the Reformation, we find at least six roots that still are important today.

1. Piety. Exemplified in the piety of Bernard of Clairvaux, piety was in existence prior to Bernard, but it is most clearly seen in his life and ministry. This then is the same piety that was renewed during the time of the Puritans.

2. Strong Biblical Leadership. The lessons learned from the disasters of the Roman Catholic Church history prove that without strong biblical leadership a church will fail.

3. Gospel as the Heart of Religion. Peter Waldo placed great emphasis on the Gospel as the heart of religion.

4. Bible Translations in All Languages. Wycliffe insisted that all people must have the Bible translated into their own language.

5. Authority of Scripture Over All Else. Hus stressed the authority of Scripture over all else (including individuals and councils). This root is emphasized many, many times throughout this history.

6. Representative Government. The Conciliar Movement focused on the importance of representative government in all spheres, including the church.

I find it quite "mind blowing" as our youth might say that there existed even prior to the Reformation these six important issues that I would consider to be *roots* of the PCA.

From Chapter Two and the beginnings of the Protestant Reformation, we find several more roots.

7. Priesthood of Believers. This allows individuals to seek truth from the Bible, but also recognizes that even the seeking was under the authority of the Scriptures to determine truth.

8. Sphere Sovereignty. While many believe that Kuyper developed this theory, it truly was born out of the Protestant Reformation.

9. Sovereign Providence of God. God is in control of all events in history, working through circumstances.

And of course, from Chapter Three and Luther we find:

10. Justification by Faith Alone Through Grace Alone. The heart of the Reformation theology remains the heart of any true church. While I mentioned it in Chapter Two, it really belongs to Luther's history.

11. Clear Conversion. This refers to the absolute necessity of a clear conversion for every Christian, or to "be reborn" as Luther related it (and by which terminology it has been referred to ever since.)

12. Proper Understanding of Works. Works are useless for conversion, but necessary as evidence of salvation.

Roots from Calvin and Chapter Four are not as many as one might think. He was essentially a systematician rather than the purveyor of new ideas. However, the one root I see from him is a crucial one. But first, we start with Zwingli:

13. Regulative Principle of Worship. This root is another one that we see emphasized (and de-emphasized) over the years.

14. Baptism of Infants. The biblical truth of the Covenant results in the baptism of infants.

Now, on to Calvin's influence:

15. Rule by Elders. Of course, this refers to oversight by multiple elders, not just one. While many credit Knox with the invention of this Presbyterian system, we must lay it at the feet of Calvin, who is the one from whom Knox learned it.

16. Sacrament of the Lord's Supper. I would also ascribe to John Calvin the essential nature and great importance of the Sacrament of the Lord's Supper.

As we turn to Chapter Five and following, we begin to see fewer and fewer new roots emerging but rather a return to the emphasis on those roots that had been diminished in importance. However, there are a few things that I believe are significant enough to be classified as a root, such as:

17. Martyrdom for the Faith. The definite willingness to be a martyr for the faith is a root of the PCA. I can't wait to hear the evaluations of that root today!

18. Fencing of the Table. The practice of prohibiting those outside the Church from celebrating the Sacrament of the Lord's Supper is a mark of the PCA.

19. Expository Preaching. Perhaps Knox's greatest gift to the church was the importance of preaching through biblical texts in a consecutive and detailed manner. (I place it here because I believe Calvin viewed his expository work as teaching. Knox may also have discerned the importance from the work of Zwingli as well.)

20. Doctrines of Grace. These doctrines include (but are not limited to) the responses to the Synod of Dordt which have come to be known as the Five Points of Calvinism.

21. Purity of the Church. While other Puritan principles are dealt with in earlier roots, I would include at this point their position on the purity of the Church as a root.

22. Presbyterian Form of Church Government. From Westminster and from Scotland alike, one of our roots is the acknowledgement that the Bible teaches this form of Church Government.

23. Confession of Faith. Also from Westminster, we value having a clear definition of a group's doctrinal positions.

24. Catechisms. Lastly but not necessarily in importance, from Westminster, is our commitment to the catechisms as an effective method of teaching detailed doctrines.

25. *Lex Rex* and the Covenanters. This refers to the freedom of the Church (as a body, as well as individually in civil life) from the absolute authority of kings.

Turning now to America, beginning in Chapter Nine, we find a few new roots yet being developed. Of course, some of these are smaller, feeder roots rather than major roots:

26. The American Way. I use this expression to mean the removing of the Puritan's desire to have the Church control civil government and of being a separate sphere unto itself.

27. Biblical Revival. Renewal of the commitment to biblical revival flowing from Reformed preaching and teaching came under Edwards and Whitefield, as well as a rejection of moralistic preaching.

28. Social Conscience. Developing a biblically instructed social conscience most probably began with the English Methodists.

29. Educated Clergy. The "Log College" and its heirs resulted from a commitment in America to the requirement of clergy to have an advanced education/degree.

30. Evangelistic Zeal. This stems from the New Side Presbyterians.

31. Educated Laity. Similar to our desire for an educated clergy is our distinction of educated lay leaders, who can maintain the conservatism of the church in spite of liberal-leaning clergy.

32. Princeton Theology. The tradition of conservative, Christian, Reformed and Presbyterian theology at Princeton Seminary seeks to express a

warm Evangelicalism and a high standard of scholarship.

33. Infallibility of Scripture. Our commitment to the infallibility of Scripture is an important root. (Later, the PCA would move to the more narrow commitment of inerrancy. See number 44 below.)

34. Covenant of Grace. The PCA understands the biblical covenant of grace to be the unifying theme of Scripture.

35. Commitment to Reformed Theology and Presbyterian Government. Maintaining this loyalty, assists us in overcoming the negative influences of Revivalism, the Arminian-based invitation system, and the Pentecostal movement.

36. Resistance to Both Classic Liberal Theology (in the North) and Neo-Orthodoxy (in the South). Our commitment to Reformed Theology and Presbyterian Government also helps us stand firm in this stance.

37. Commitment to Minister to Minorities. This endeavor is more than a commitment to integration of the church. In the PCA, however, this root has grown beyond its origins in the Southern church to include (to an ever-growing degree) ministry to minorities in our midst.

38. High View of the Role of Ruling Elders. We continue to develop the importance of educated and ordained laity.

39. Biblical Discipline. Our commitment to this principle is an important root. (While this could have

been listed under the Swiss Reformation, it was in the 20th Century American church that its importance was highlighted and became universally accepted as the third mark of the church.)

40. Conservatism. In our context, this is described by a willingness to separate from ungodliness, from liberal theology at the leadership of the denomination, and most especially from the unwillingness to apply biblical discipline when needed (i.e., to be willing to apply biblical discipline in order to restore a member to fellowship with Christ and the Church.)

41. Commitment to the Fundamentals of the Faith. Without being Fundamentalists (a term which carries negative connotations in the midst of our culture), the PCA strives to maintain committed to the essentials of the Christian faith.

42. Development of Multiple Seminaries Teaching Reformed Theology. The increase of credible seminaries has long been a focus of endeavor.

43. Uniting of Former Divisions. The PCA is actively expresses a willingness to join with other Presbyterian and Reformed churches when there is agreement on biblical principles.

44. Commitment to Biblical Inerrancy. In the latter half of the 20th Century, some evangelicals rejected inerrancy, choosing to believe in the infallibility of Scripture (as defined in the Westminster Confession of Faith) even though they supposed errors in the Bible.

45. Separate Oversight of Denominational Ministries. The development of financially separate

oversight committees (rather than having a combined treasury at the general assembly level) is unique to the PCA. Each ministry is dependent on church and individual support to carry out its denominationally assigned work.

46. "Two Office" Perspective. The PCA was the first denomination to constitutionally sanction two offices of church government: Elder (divided into the two classes: "Teaching" and "Ruling") and Deacon.

47. Unique Role of Women's Ministry. Our roots include the development of a strong women's ministry while at the same time defending our commitment to the biblical principal that only men are ordained to church office.

48. Publication of Reformed and Covenantal Educational Materials. Recognizing the need for carefully developed materials, the PCA has assured their production through a joint venture/partnership (known as Great Commission Publications) with the Orthodox Presbyterian Church.

49. High View of Ordination Vows. We take seriously the vows taken by our officers, including a "Good Faith" subscription (adherence) to the constitutional standards of the church. This form of subscription allows defined areas of approved differences, in the form of declared exceptions stated to the presbytery or church that ordains the officer.

50. The Great Commission. Our commitment to following the Lord's command in Matthew 28:18-20 has resulted in our developing the largest force of Presbyterian missionaries in the history of the world.

Without a doubt, justification by faith and biblical inerrancy are primary roots, while others are small, growing, feeder roots. And yet, others are somewhere in between. They are simply listed in the order presented in the chapters of this book.

Now, as to my call for responses, I would be pleased to receive from any elder in the PCA a response (short or long) which discusses the health of these roots today. Perhaps, you would differ with some of the listings and/or suggest the addition of other possible roots. Those received by September 1, 2006 may be considered for publication in a separate volume and/or disseminated on-line. (Please send email responses in a Word document attachment to *don@metokos.org*.)

As the title of this chapter suggests, my desire is to get you thinking about our roots the way a scientist who is skilled in identifying the nature, origin, progress and cause of disease would examine a tissue specimen. I hope you have gained an expanded knowledge of the sacrifice and service of the saints that have gone before, as well as a deeper appreciation of the importance of the particular history that makes up the roots of the PCA—those aspects which make us "who we are." At the very least, I hope you can now see the importance of a basic understanding of "times gone by" so that certain mistakes are not, by God's grace, repeated in the future. We must maintain our commitment to the standards and principles for which many of our forefathers died, and in so doing, leave a solid legacy for those who will come after.

## *About the Author*

Dr. Clements was ordained in July of 1974 in the National Presbyterian Church (the original name of the PCA). After several years as a pastor in Central Georgia Presbytery, he returned to the U.S. Navy, where he had previously spent twelve years on active duty prior to entering seminary. Having left as an enlisted man (Chief Petty Officer), he returned as a Navy Chaplain.

Serving ten additional years on active duty on assignments with Destroyer Squadrons in San Diego; at the Naval Air Station in Pensacola; as Chaplain for a nuclear-powered guided missile cruiser and a submarine tender in Norfolk, and finally as Chaplain of the Naval Hospital, Newport, RI, Don retired in 1985.

For the next eighteen years, he pastored two "turn-around" church revitalizations of small churches in Blacksburg and Narrows, VA. On January 1, 2003 he moved full-time into a ministry he had developed called *Metokos Ministries— Encouragement for Small Churches.* Affiliated with the Presbyterian Evangelistic Fellowship (PEF) as an evangelist, Don works with small churches (mostly under 100 members) that need encouragement and resources to develop vision plans, go through pulpit transitions, and other specific needs. (Visit his website at *www.metokos.org.*)

Don holds an M.Div. (with honors) from Covenant Theological Seminary in St. Louis, and a D.Min. (in Adult Education) from Gordon Conwell Theological Seminary in South Hamilton, MA. He and his wife, Esther, live with their Cocker Spaniel "Shadow" in their newly remodeled retirement home in the Appalachian Mountain town of Narrows, Virginia, and they spend lots of time visiting their three grown daughters who currently live in Mississippi, South Dakota and Virginia.

Printed in the United States
48655LVS00003B/223-243

9 780974 233178